Ready® | 6 Mathematics
Common Core | INSTRUCTION

W9-CND-035

Project Manager: Amy Chen
Revising Editor: Paul Meyers
Supervising Editor: Fran Fanning
Cover Designer and Illustrator: Julia Bourque
Book Design: Scott Hoffman

NOT FOR RESALE

Table of Contents

Unit 1: Ratios and Proportional Relationships 1

CCSS

Lesson 1 Ratios . . . . .2 — 6.RP.A.1

Lesson 2 *Understand* Unit Rate . . . . 10 — 6.RP.A.2

Lesson 3 Equivalent Ratios . . . . 16 — 6.RP.A.3a

Lesson 4 Solve Problems with Unit Rate . . . . 26 — 6.RP.A.3b, 6.RP.A.3d

Lesson 5 Solve Problems with Percent . . . . 38 — 6.RP.A.3c

Unit 1 Interim Assessment 48

Unit 2: The Number System 51

Lesson 6 *Understand* Division with Fractions . . . . .52 — 6.NS.A.1

Lesson 7 Divide with Fractions. . . . . .58 — 6.NS.A.1

Lesson 8 Divide Multi-Digit Numbers . . . . 70 — 6.NS.B.2

Lesson 9 Add and Subtract Decimals. . . . . .80 — 6.NS.B.3

Lesson 10 Multiply and Divide Decimals . . . . .90 — 6.NS.B.3

Lesson 11 Common Factors and Multiples . . . . 102 — 6.NS.B.4

Lesson 12 *Understand* Positive and Negative Numbers . . . . 112 — 6.NS.C.5, 6.NS.C.6a, 6.NS.C.6c

Lesson 13 Absolute Value and Ordering Numbers . . . . 118 — 6.NS.C.5, 6.NS.C.7a, 6.NS.C.7b, 6.NS.C.7c, 6.NS.C.7d

Lesson 14 The Coordinate Plane . . . . 128 — 6.NS.C.6b, 6.NS.C.6c, 6.NS.C.8

Unit 2 Interim Assessment 140

Unit 3: Expressions and Equations 143

Lesson 15 Numerical Expressions with Exponents . . . . 144 — 6.EE.A.1

Lesson 16 Algebraic Expressions . . . . 154 — 6.EE.A.2a, 6.EE.A.2b, 6.EE.A.2c

Lesson 17 Equivalent Expressions . . . . 166 — 6.EE.A.3, 6.EE.A.4

Lesson 18 *Understand* Solutions to Equations. . . . . 178 — 6.EE.B.5

Lesson 19 Solve Equations . . . . 184 — 6.EE.B.6, 6.EE.B.7

Table of Contents

Unit 3: Expressions and Equations *(continued)*

CCSS

Lesson 20 Solve Inequalities 196   6.EE.B.5, 6.EE.B.8

Lesson 21 Dependent and Independent Variables 206   6.EE.C.9

Unit 3 Interim Assessment 216

Unit 4: Geometry 219

Lesson 22 Area of Polygons 220   6.G.A.1

Lesson 23 Polygons in the Coordinate Plane 230   6.G.A.3

Lesson 24 Nets and Surface Area 240   6.G.A.4

Lesson 25 Volume 252   6.G.A.2

Unit 4 Interim Assessment 262

Unit 5: Statistics and Probability 265

Lesson 26 *Understand* Statistical Questions 266   6.SP.A.1

Lesson 27 Measures of Center and Variability 272   6.SP.A.2, 6.SP.A.3

Lesson 28 Display Data on Dot Plots, Histograms, and Box Plots . . . 284   6.SP.B.4

Lesson 29 Analyze Numerical Data 296   6.SP.B.5a, 6.SP.B.5b, 6.SP.B.5c, 6.SP.B.5d

Unit 5 Interim Assessment 306

Common Core State Standards for Mathematics, Grade 6 309

Unit 1
Ratios and Proportional Relationships

Have you ever gone to the store to buy some juice and found a price label like this?

Twenty four cents for a bottle of juice? You decide to buy 10 bottles! Unfortunately, you will have to pay $3.69 for this bottle of juice. The 24.3¢ is the unit price. Knowing about rates and ratios will help you buy your juice and solve problems about percent, measurements, and speeds.

$3.69

24.3¢ per oz

✓ Self Check

Before starting this unit, check off the skills you know below. As you complete each lesson, see how many more you can check off!

I can:	Before this unit	After this unit
write a ratio to describe the relationship between two quantities	☐	☐
find the rate and unit rate associated with a given ratio	☐	☐
compare ratios and find equivalent ratios	☐	☐
solve unit rate problems	☐	☐
solve percent problems	☐	☐

Lesson 1   Part 1: Introduction

Ratios

You already know that a fraction is a way to compare a part to a whole. Take a look at this problem.

Carlos has 4 tennis balls and 5 baseballs.

How can you compare the number of each type of ball to the total number of balls?
How can you compare the number of one type to the number of the other type?

Explore It

Use the math you already know to solve the problem.

● What fraction of the balls are tennis balls? _____

● What fraction of the balls are baseballs? _____

● You can also compare two quantities with words. You can write the numerical comparison of 4 tennis balls to 9 total as simply 4 *to* 9. Write a comparison of the number of baseballs to the number of total balls, using the word *to*.

_____

● You can also use a colon (:) to separate quantities when you compare numbers. Use this notation to compare the number of each type of ball to the total. _____

● How does each of these notations, $\frac{4}{9}$, 4 to 9, and 4:9, compare the number of tennis balls to the total number of balls?

_____

_____

Find Out More

A **ratio** is a way to compare two different quantities.

Sometimes you compare the two parts.

> 4 tennis balls to 5 baseballs
>
> 5 baseballs to 4 tennis balls

Sometimes you compare the part and the whole amount.

> 4 tennis balls to 9 balls
>
> 5 baseballs to 9 balls

To write a ratio you can use the word "to," a colon, or a fraction bar. The expressions *4 to 5, 4:5,* and $\frac{4}{5}$ all represent the ratio of 4 compared to 5.

There are many ways to compare the number of balls Carlos has.

Part to Part	Part to Whole	Whole to Part
tennis balls to baseballs 4 to 5 4:5 $\frac{4}{5}$	tennis balls to total balls 4 to 9 4:9 $\frac{4}{9}$	total balls to tennis balls 9 to 4 9:4 $\frac{9}{4}$
baseballs to tennis balls 5 to 4 5:4 $\frac{5}{4}$	baseballs to total balls 5 to 9 5:9 $\frac{5}{9}$	total balls to baseballs 9 to 5 9:5 $\frac{9}{5}$
You can also use the phrases "for each" and "for every" to describe ratios. For example: 4 tennis balls for every 5 baseballs. 4 tennis balls for each set of 5 baseballs.		

Reflect

1 Suppose Carlos was given a basketball. What is the ratio of tennis balls to baseballs? _____ What is the ratio of total balls to tennis balls? _____ Compare the ratios before Carlos got the basketball and after he got it. How did the basketball affect the ratios?

_____

_____

Read the problem below. Then explore different ways to compare quantities using ratios.

Chris mixes 4 cups of cereal, 3 cups of pecans, and 2 cups of raisins to make a snack mix. How can you use ratios to compare the quantities of each ingredient and the total amount of snack mix?

 **Picture It**

You can use a diagram to represent the information in the problem.

Cereal   Pecans   Raisins

Model It

You can use a tape diagram to help you see how the amounts of ingredients compare to one another and to the total amount.

To show how the ingredients compare, represent each cup with a rectangle. Then line up the rectangles for each ingredient in a row.

Cereal				
Pecans			
Raisins		
Total mix									

Connect It

Now you will solve the problem from the previous page using ratios to compare the quantities.

2 What are three ways to write the ratio of cups of cereal to cups of pecans?

_____

3 Does the ratio of cereal to pecans compare part to part, part to whole, or whole

to part? _____

4 What is the total amount of snack mix? _____

5 Write ratios to compare the amount of each ingredient to the total amount of snack

mix. _____

6 Explain how you can write a ratio to compare two different quantities.

_____

_____

_____

Try It

Use what you learned about writing ratios to solve these problems.

7 Leo blew up 7 balloons. Kathy blew up 5 balloons. Write each ratio in at least
two different ways.

ratio of Kathy's balloons to Leo's balloons _____

ratio of Leo's balloons to Kathy's balloons _____

ratio of total balloons to Leo's balloons _____

8 Each class has the goal of selling 100 tickets to the school carnival. Miss Garcia's class
sells 87 tickets. Mr. Carpenter's class sells 113 tickets. Write each ratio in at least two
different ways.

ratio of Miss Garcia's sales to the goal _____

ratio of Mr. Carpenter's sales to the goal _____

ratio of Mr. Carpenter's sales to Miss Garcia's sales _____

The student used a tape diagram to show the total pieces of fruit and the number of students in the study group.

Study the model below. Then solve problems 9–11.

Student Model

Ahmad's mom prepares a plate with 5 peaches and 4 apples for the 6 students in Ahmad's study group. What is the ratio of fruit to students?

Look at how you could show your work using a diagram.

Fruits		P	P	P	P	P	A	A	A	A
Students		S	S	S	S	S	S			

Solution: Add 5 + 4 = 9; there are 9 pieces of fruit in all. There are 6 students. The ratio of fruit to students is 9 to 6. The ratio can also be written as 9:6 and $\frac{9}{6}$.

💬**Pair/Share**

If the students shared all of the fruit equally, how many pieces would each student receive?

Are you looking for a part to part, a part to whole, or a whole to part ratio?

9 Kaya received these ribbons at swim meets. What is the ratio of first-place ribbons to third-place ribbons?

💬**Pair/Share**

Suppose Kaya won two more second-place ribbons. How would the ratio change?

Solution: _____

10 Ms. Powell's class voted on where to go for a field trip. The museum received 11 votes, and 16 students voted to go to the aquarium. Use numbers and words to write the ratio of votes for the aquarium to votes for the museum.

Remember to pay close attention to the order of the quantities in the ratio.

Solution: _____

_____

_____

Pair/Share

Suppose 3 students who voted to go to the aquarium changed their votes to the museum. How would the ratio change?

11 Donnie's dog had a litter of puppies. He notices that 2 are brown, 1 is white, and 3 are spotted. What is the ratio of total puppies to brown puppies? Circle the letter of the correct answer.

A 2:6

B 2:4

C 4:2

D 6:2

Anya chose **A** as the correct answer. How did she get that answer?

What are the two quantities that need to be included in the ratio?

_____

_____

_____

_____

Pair/Share

What are some other ratios you can write with the information given in the problem?

Solve the problems.

1 Percy's Pizza Parlor sells three sizes of pizza. What is the ratio of the diameter of the large pizza to the diameter of the medium pizza?

Size	Diameter
Small	11 in.
Medium	14 in.
Large	17 in.

A 14 to 17

B 17:11

C $\frac{17}{14}$

D 3:14

2 Rita reads 3 times as many fiction books as non-fiction books. What is the ratio of fiction books to total books?

A 1:4

B 3 to 4

C 4 to 3

D 3:1

3 The ratio of girls to boys in a student basketball league is 5:6. Choose True or False for each statement.

A For every 5 girls in the league, there are 6 boys. ☐ True ☐ False

B For every 6 girls in the league, there are 5 boys. ☐ True ☐ False

C There are exactly 11 students in the league. ☐ True ☐ False

D The ratio of girls to total students in the league is 5:11. ☐ True ☐ False

4　Of the 15 children at the park, 12 children are riding bicycles and 3 children are riding scooters. Which ratio is correct? Circle all that apply.

A　The ratio of bicycles to scooters is 12 to 3.

B　The ratio of scooters to children is 3 to 15.

C　The ratio of bicycles to children is 4 to 5.

D　The ratio of scooters to children is 9 to 12.

E　The ratio of bicycles to children is 12 to 3.

5　Haley buys 8 apples for $3 and 3 bananas for $1. What is the ratio of the number of pieces of fruit she buys to the total dollars she spends? Write the answer in at least 2 different ways.

Answer _____

6　In the talent show, 6 students plan to sing, 7 students plan to dance, and 2 students plan to tell jokes. Rick said that the ratio of singers to joke-tellers is 6 to 2. Leah said that the ratio of joke-tellers to singers is 1 to 3. Who is correct? Explain why.

_____

_____

_____

_____

_____

✓ **Self Check**　*Go back and see what you can check off on the Self Check on page 1.*

Lesson 2   Part 1: Introduction 👥

Understand Unit Rate

How are ratios, rates, and unit rates related?

Ratios, rates, and **unit rates** are all comparisons. They compare one quantity to another quantity.

A **ratio** compares any two quantities.

Yolanda uses 4 cups of nuts and 2 cups of dried fruit to make trail mix.

You can use a tape diagram to show this comparison.

nuts

dried fruit

The ratio is 4 cups to 2 cups or 4:2. Notice that the quantity of nuts is double the quantity of dried fruit.

🔍 **Think**   Every ratio has a related rate.

nuts

dried fruit

A related **rate** is an equivalent ratio that compares the first quantity in a ratio to only one of the second quantity. In this example, you know that the amount of nuts is double the amount of dried fruit. So, what if you wanted the same kind of mix but only used 1 cup of dried fruit? How many cups of nuts would you use?

Think: 4:2 is the same as _____:1?

Think: What number is 1 doubled?

The rate is 2 cups of nuts to 1 cup of dried fruit. You can also say the rate is 2 cups of nuts per cup of fruit.

🔍 **Think** Every rate has a related unit rate.

The **unit rate** is the part of the rate that is being compared to 1. In the previous problem, the unit rate of nuts to fruit is 2. Let's look at another example.

Marco earned $85 for 10 hours of work.

Ratio of dollars to hours: 85 to 10

Rate of dollars to 1 hour: Marco earned $85 in 10 hours, so he earned $85 ÷ 10 in 1 hour. He earned $8.50 for each 1 hour, or $8.50 per 1 hour.

Unit Rate: The number part of the rate 8.50 dollars per hour is 8.50.

Marco earned $8.50 for each hour that he worked.

> *Talking about rates in different ways helps me understand them. I can say "$8.50 for every hour," "$8.50 for each hour," or "$8.50 per hour."*

✏️ **Reflect**

1 What is the difference between a ratio and its related rate and unit rate?

_____

_____

_____

Explore It

A double number line can be used to find rate and unit rate.

A car can travel 300 miles on 10 gallons of gas. The ratio is 300 miles to 10 gallons.

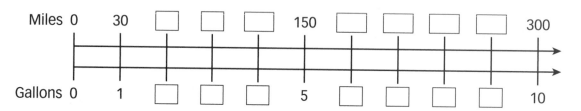

2 What do the 300 and 10 in the diagram represent?

_____

3 How many gallons does each section along the bottom number line represent?

_____ Fill in the remaining numbers on the bottom number line.

4 Look at the corresponding pairs of numbers on the bottom and top number lines. Write a multiplication sentence to show how 10 gallons and 300 miles are related. How are 5 gallons and 150 miles related? How are 1 gallon and 30 miles related?

_____

5 Use words to describe the relationship between the number of miles and each corresponding number of gallons.

_____

_____

6 Fill in the remaining numbers on the number line. What is the rate of miles per gallon for this car?

_____

7 What is the unit rate of miles to gallons? _____

💬 Talk About It

Solve the problems below as a group.

8 Look at the model on the previous page. What pattern do you see in the numbers of miles?

_____

What pattern do you see in the number of gallons?

_____

9 Now look at all of the corresponding numbers of miles and gallons. Describe the pattern.

_____

_____

10 Write the ratio given in the problem. _____ Divide both quantities in the ratio by the second quantity in the ratio and write a new ratio. What is this ratio called? Explain. _____

_____

11 Look at your answer to Problem 10. How can you find the related rate for a ratio?

_____

✏️ Try It Another Way

Work with your group to use equivalent fractions to find the rate and unit rate.

12 A 10-pound box of apples costs $12.50. Write the ratio of cost to number of pounds as a fraction. Then find an equivalent fraction with a denominator of 1. Write the rate and unit rate to describe the cost of the apples.

_____

_____

13 A driver traveled 260 miles on the highway for 4 hours, driving at the same speed for the whole trip. Write the ratio of miles to hours. Then use what you know about equivalent fractions to write a related rate and unit rate.

_____

_____

Connect It

Talk through these problems as a class, then write your answers below.

14 Identify: Write the letter of the rate that matches each ratio.

$7.50 : 3 pounds _____	a. $0.75 for every 1 pound
$3.75 to 5 pounds _____	b. $2.25 for each 1 pound
$6.00 : 4 pounds _____	c. $2.50 for every 1 pound
$13.50 to 6 pounds _____	d. $1.50 per 1 pound

15 Analyze: Use the information on this nutrition label to write the unit rates described below. Show your work.

NUTRITION FACTS
Serving Size 2 Crackers (14 grams)
Servings Per Container: About 20

Amount Per Serving
Calories 50   Calories From Fat 15

There are _____ calories in 1 cracker.

One cracker has a mass of _____ grams.

There are _____ fat calories in 1 cracker.

_____

_____

_____

16 Compare: Dawn earned $97.50 for 10 hours of work. Amy earned $120 for 12 hours of work. How much did each person earn per hour? How can you use this information to compare their earnings?

_____

_____

_____

_____

💡 Put It Together

17 A recipe uses 3 cups of flour and 2 cups of sugar.

A Write the ratio of cups of flour to cups of sugar as a fraction: _____ cups.

Divide the first quantity by the second quantity to find the related rate:

_____ cups ÷ _____ cups = _____ cups to _____ cup.

The unit rate is _____.

B Now write a ratio of cups of sugar to cups of flour as a fraction: _____ cups.

Divide the first quantity by the second quantity to find the related rate:

_____ cups ÷ _____ cups = _____ cups to _____ cup.

The unit rate is _____.

C Imagine that the recipe is doubled and that 4 cups of sugar are used. Use the unit rate in A to find how much flour is needed if the recipe is made with 4 cups of sugar. Show your work.

_____

_____

D Imagine that 6 cups of flour are used to make the recipe. Use the unit rate in B to find how much sugar is needed if the recipe is made with 6 cups of flour.

_____

_____

E Compare your answers to C and D and explain how the two unit rates are related.

_____

_____

_____

_____

Lesson 3   Part 1: Introduction

Equivalent Ratios

In Lessons 1 and 2, you learned about ratios. Take a look at this problem.

Mr. West uses this recipe to make a batch of soup. He often doubles or triples the recipe and freezes some of the soup. What ratio of cups of stock to batches of soup should Mr. West use to make 1, 2, and 3 batches of soup?

SOUP INGREDIENTS

1 Pound Potatoes
2 Leeks
2 Cups Chopped Onion
4 Cups Stock
1 Tablespoon Olive Oil
1 Teaspoon Italian Seasoning

Explore It

Use math you already know to solve the problem.

How many cups of stock are needed to double the recipe? Explain.

_____

_____

How many cups of stock are needed to triple the recipe? Explain.

_____

_____

Write the ratios of cups of stock to batches of soup for 1, 2, and 3 batches of soup.

_____

_____

Find the related rate and unit rate for each ratio. Remember, you divide the first quantity by the second to find the related rate. What do you notice about all of the rates and unit rates? _____

_____

_____

_____

Find Out More

The ratios of cups of stock to batches of soup that you wrote in Explore It are **equivalent ratios**. They all have the same related rate and unit rate. Each ratio of cups of stock to batches of soup has a unit rate of 4. The first quantity (cups of stock) in each ratio is 4 times the second quantity (batches of soup).

You can make a table to show other equivalent ratios.

Cups of Stock	4	8	12	16	20	24	28
Batches of Soup	1	2	3	4	5	6	7

If you know a ratio, you can make a table with as many equivalent ratios as you want.

In the problem on the previous page, the ratio that was given was a rate: 4 cups of stock to 1 batch of soup. Many problems give a ratio that is not expressed as a rate.

A caterer prepares fruit bowls for a luncheon. Each bowl has 8 grapes for every 3 strawberries.

	8×1	8×2	8×3	8×4	8×5
Number of Grapes	8	16	24	32	40
Number of Strawberries	3	6	9	12	15
	3×1	3×2	3×3	3×4	3×5

The ratio of grapes to strawberries in each fruit bowl is 8 to 3. You can write other ratios equivalent to 8 to 3 using multiplication.

Reflect

1. How can you write equivalent ratios?

_____

_____

_____

Read the problem below. Then explore different ways to show equivalent ratios.

A cafeteria worker knows that it takes 3 bottles of juice to serve a table of 18 students. How many bottles of juice are needed for 24 students? How many bottles of juice are needed for 42 students?

🔍 Picture It

You can draw a diagram to represent a ratio of 18 students to 3 bottles of juice.

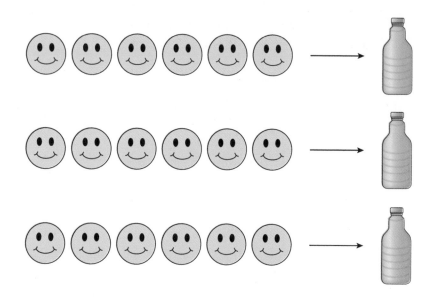

🔍 Model It

You can also make a table to show ratios of the number of students to the number of bottles of juice.

Number of Students	6	12	18				
Bottles of Juice	1	2	3	4	5	6	7

Connect It

Now you will use the diagram and the table to solve the problem.

2 What is the ratio of the number of students to the number of bottles of juice?

_____

3 What is the related rate for this ratio? Explain how the diagram represents this.

_____

_____

_____

4 Look at the table. What is the unit rate? Tell how you know.

_____

_____

5 Use the unit rate to complete the table. How many bottles are needed for 24 and 42

students? _____

6 How do you use a table to show equivalent ratios? _____

_____

_____

_____

Try It

**Use what you learned to solve these problems. Show your work on a separate
sheet of paper.**

7 Mikaela travels 15 blocks on her skateboard in 5 minutes. At this speed, how many
blocks can she travel on her skateboard in 12 minutes? _____

8 A seamstress uses 12 yards of fabric to make 3 costumes for students in the chorus.
How many yards will she need to make costumes for all 25 students in the chorus?

_____

Read the problem below. Then explore different ways to show equivalent ratios.

A 4-ounce serving of yogurt has 8 grams of protein. How many grams of protein are in a 10-ounce serving? How many grams of protein are in the whole 16-ounce container of yogurt?

 **Model It**

You can use a table to show equivalent ratios.

Ounces of Yogurt	1	4	8	10	12	14	16
Grams of Protein	2	8	16	20	24	28	32

Graph It

You can plot the ordered pairs on the coordinate plane.

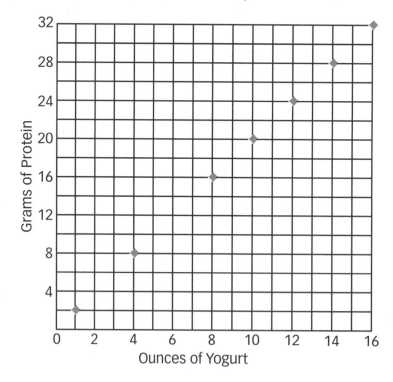

Connect It

Now you will explore how to use the table and graph to find equivalent ratios.

9 What is the ratio of ounces of yogurt to grams of protein?

_____

10 Look at the table. How many grams of protein are in 1 ounce of yogurt?

_____

11 Each point on the graph shows an ordered pair from the table. Fill in the blanks to show these ordered pairs.

(1,____)   (4, 8)   (10,____)   (16,____)

12 How are the numbers in each ordered pair related?

_____

13 The ordered pair (10, 20) means 10 ounces of yogurt to ____ grams of protein.

The ordered pair (16, 32) means ____ ounces of yogurt to ____ grams of protein.

14 The table and graph show equivalent ratios. How are they similar? How are they different?

_____

_____

_____

Try It

Use what you just learned to solve these problems. Show your work on a separate sheet of paper.

15 On in-line skates, Bradley skates 4 miles in 20 minutes. At this speed, how long would it take him to skate the entire length of a 12-mile bike path? _____

16 The cost of 5 team sweatshirts is $90. At this price, how much would it cost to buy sweatshirts for a whole team of 15 players? _____

Study the model below. Then solve problems 17–19.

The student made tables of equivalent ratios for Jake's recipe and Ally's recipe. You can compare the ratios.

> *Student Model*
>
> Jake made hummingbird nectar by mixing 8 cups of water with 2 cups of sugar. Ally used 9 cups of water and 3 cups of sugar. Which recipe is more sugary? Explain why.
>
> **Look at how you could show your work using tables.**
>
> Jake's Recipe
>
> | Cups of water | 4 | 8 |
> |---|---|---|
> | Cups of sugar | 1 | 2 |
>
> Ally's Recipe
>
> | Cups of water | 3 | 9 |
> |---|---|---|
> | Cups of sugar | 1 | 3 |
>
> Look at the ratios that compare the cups of water to 1 cup of sugar. Ally's recipe has a ratio of 3 cups of water to 1 cup of sugar. Jake's recipe has a ratio of 4 cups of water to 1 cup of sugar.
>
> Solution: _Since Ally's recipe has less water for the same amount of sugar, her recipe is more sugary._

💬**Pair/Share**

How could you use division to solve the problem?

What is the ratio of students to pizzas?

17 Mrs. Silva orders 5 pizzas for every 20 students working on the campus clean-up. How many pizzas should she order if 36 students participate? How many pizzas should she order if 48 students participate?

Show your work.

💬**Pair/Share**

How would the problem change if Mrs. Silva orders 6 pizzas for 20 students?

Solution: _____

18 David wants to fill his backyard swimming pool. His garden hose delivers 40 gallons in 5 minutes. How many gallons of water will be in the pool after 20 minutes? After 1 hour?

Show your work.

How many minutes are in 1 hour?

Solution: _____

◯ Pair/Share

How could you use the unit rate to solve the problem?

19 Coach McCarthy bought 6 soccer balls for $150. Which table correctly shows equivalent ratios for this cost?

A

Number of Balls	1	2	3	4	5	6
Cost	$0	$30	$60	$90	$120	$150

B

Number of Balls	1	2	3	4	5	6
Cost	$25	$50	$75	$100	$125	$150

C

Number of Balls	1	2	3	4	5	6
Cost	$20	$40	$60	$80	$100	$150

D

Number of Balls	1	2	3	4	5	6
Cost	$120	$126	$132	$138	$144	$150

What is the relationship between the cost and the number of soccer balls?

Kristin chose **C** as the correct answer. How did she get this answer?

_____

_____

_____

_____

◯ Pair/Share

How can you use division to find which table shows equivalent ratios?

Solve the problems.

1 Which table shows equivalent ratios?

A

Number of Raisins	1	2	3	4	5	6
Total Calories	5	6	7	8	9	10

B

Number of Raisins	1	2	3	4	5	6
Total Calories	5	7	8	9	10	11

C

Number of Raisins	1	2	3	4	5	6
Total Calories	5	10	15	20	25	30

D

Number of Raisins	1	2	3	4	5	6
Total Calories	5	12	21	32	45	60

2 The table shows the calories in different numbers of small tangerines. Which expression does NOT show a way to find the number of calories in 10 tangerines?

Tangerines	2	4	6	8
Calories	80	160	240	320

A 10×20

B 10×40

C $80 + 320$

D $160 + 240$

3 Mrs. Baca uses a phone card to call her relatives in Colombia. It costs her 45 cents to talk for 15 minutes. Choose True or False for each statement.

A For 75 cents, Mrs. Baca can talk for 3 minutes. ☐ True ☐ False

B The call rate is 3 cents per minute. ☐ True ☐ False

C The call rate can be represented by the ratio 45:15. ☐ True ☐ False

D Divide 75 by 15 to find the number of minutes Mrs. Baca can talk. ☐ True ☐ False

4   Christina wants to buy some miniature goldfish. She reads that a 9-gallon aquarium is the right size for 3 miniature goldfish. The graph represents this relationship.

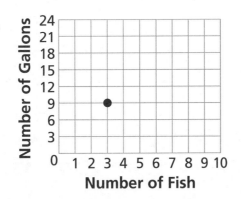

Which points show equivalent ratios that would also be on the graph? Select all that apply.

A   (6, 18)   **C**   (4, 10)

B   (6, 12)   **D**   (1, 3)

5   Gloria rides a bike 8 miles in 40 minutes. Nanette rides a bike 5 miles in 30 minutes. Who will bike the farthest in 1 hour? How much farther?

Show your work.

_____

_____

6   One recipe for cereal bars uses 5 cups of cereal and $2\frac{1}{2}$ cups of nuts. A different recipe uses 3 cups of cereal and 1 cup of nuts. Which recipe is more nutty?

Show your work.

_____

_____

✓ **Self Check**   *Go back and see what you can check off on the Self Check on page 1.*

Lesson 4   Part 1: Introduction 👥

Solve Problems with Unit Rate

CCSS
6.RP.A.3b
6.RP.A.3d

In Lesson 3 you learned to use tables to work with equivalent ratios. Take a look at this problem.

Karalee paints magnets that she sells at craft fairs. She can paint 12 magnets in 4 hours. At this rate, how many magnets can she paint in 2 hours? In 10 hours?

🔍 Explore It

Use the math you already know to solve the problem.

Magnets		6	12		30
Hours	1		4	8	

▪ What is the ratio of magnets to hours? _____

▪ What ratio do you get if you double the number of magnets and hours?

_____ Write your answer in the table.

▪ How long would it take to paint 6 magnets? How do you know? _____

_____

_____ Fill in the table with this ratio.

▪ You know how long it takes to paint 24 magnets and 6 magnets. How can you use

that information to calculate how long it takes her to paint 30 magnets? _____

_____

_____ Fill in the table with this ratio.

▪ Explain how you can use the information in the table to find out how many magnets she

can paint in 1 hour. _____

_____

▪ Fill in the table with this ratio.

Find Out More

A table is one way to show the relationship between the number of magnets and the time it takes to paint them. A double number line also shows the relationship.

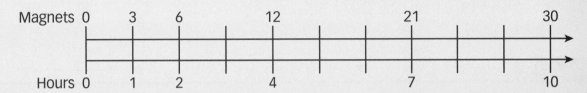

Notice that the mark for 6 magnets is halfway between 0 and 12 and the line for 2 hours is halfway between 0 and 4 hours. You can use halves again to find the rate of 3 magnets in 1 hour.

Once you find that the unit rate is 3, you can multiply or divide to find other equivalent ratios.

Divide the number of magnets by 3 to find how long Karalee will take to complete them.

number of magnets ÷ unit rate = hours
30 ÷ 3 = 10

Karalee will take 10 hours to paint 30 magnets.

Multiply the number of hours by 3 to find how many magnets Karalee can paint in that time.

hours • unit rate = total magnets
7 • 3 = 21

Karalee can paint 21 magnets in 7 hours.

Reflect

1 Explain and show how to use the unit rate to find the missing numbers on the double number line.

_____

_____

_____

Read the problem below. Then explore different ways to solve a problem involving unit price.

> Isabella buys 4 pounds of tomatoes for $6.00. How much do 7 pounds of tomatoes cost? How much do 10 pounds of tomatoes cost?

Model It

You can use a table to help you find equivalent ratios.

You know that 4 pounds of tomatoes cost $6.00.

If you divide both quantities in this ratio by 2, you find that 2 pounds cost $3.00.

If you divide both quantities in the ratio 3 to 2 by 2, you find that 1 pound costs $1.50. This is the **unit price**, or the price for 1 unit. Here the unit happens to be pounds.

Cost ($)	1.50	3		6						
Pounds	1	2	3	4	5	6	7	8	9	10

Model It

You can add or multiply with the numbers in the table to complete the rest of it. Here is one way to find the missing values. Use this information to fill in the table.

3 pounds = 2 pounds + 1 pound. Add the corresponding costs: $3.00 + $1.50 = $4.50.

5 pounds = 2 pounds + 3 pounds. Add the corresponding costs: $3.00 + $4.50 = $7.50.

6 pounds = 2 pounds • 3. Multiply the cost of 2 pounds by 3: $3.00 • 3 = $9.00.

7 pounds = 5 pounds + 2 pounds. Add the corresponding costs: $7.50 + $3.00 = $10.50.

8 pounds = 4 pounds • 2. Multiply the cost of 4 pounds by 2: $6.00 • 2 = $12.00.

9 pounds = 4 pounds + 5 pounds. Add the corresponding costs: $6.00 + $7.50 = $13.50.

10 pounds = 1 pound • 10. Multiply the cost of 1 pound by 10: $1.50 • 10 = $15.00.

Connect It

Now you will use the unit price to solve the problem from the previous page.

2 What ratio is given in the problem? _____

3 Explain how to use this ratio to find the unit price. _____

_____

4 How can you use the unit price to find the cost of 7 pounds of tomatoes and
10 pounds of tomatoes? Find the costs.

_____

_____

5 When might you make a table of equivalent ratios to solve a problem? When might
you find the unit rate and multiplication to solve a problem?

_____

_____

_____

6 Explain how can you find the amount of tomatoes that you can buy with $18.00.

_____

_____

_____

_____

Try It

**Use what you've just learned about unit price to solve these problems. Show your
work on a separate sheet of paper.**

7 Mrs. Sisneros bought 3 yards of ribbon for $1.50. How much would 5 yards of the
same ribbon cost? _____

8 Jack bought 4 bagels for $3.00. How many bagels can he buy for $4.50? _____

Read the problem below. Then explore different ways to solve a problem involving constant speed.

> Bill drove 200 miles in 4 hours. At this speed, how long will it take him to drive 300 miles? How long will it take him to drive 400 miles?

Model It

You can show the relationship between miles and hours using a double number line.

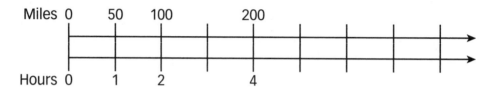

You know that in 4 hours, Bill travels 200 miles. The same vertical line is labeled with 200 miles and 4 hours. If you divide both quantities in this ratio by 2, you find that in 2 hours he travels 100 miles. Divide both quantities in the ratio 100 to 2 by 2, and you find that in 1 hour he travels 50 miles.

Model It

Here is one way you can use the quantities labeled on the double number line to complete the rest of it. Fill in the blanks below, and then finish labeling the number line.

3 hours = 2 hours + 1 hour and _____ miles = 100 miles + 50 miles.

5 hours = 2 hours + 3 hours and _____ miles = 100 miles + 150 miles.

6 hours = 2 hours • 3 and _____ miles = 100 miles • 3.

The unit rate is 50 miles for each 1 hour. Bill can drive 50 • 7, or _____ miles in 7 hours and 50 • 8, or _____ miles in 8 hours.

Connect It

9 What does the double number line show as the unit rate? _____

10 Show how to use the ratio given in the problem to find the unit rate. _____

11 How can you use the unit rate to solve the problem?

_____

_____

12 Suppose you want to know how long it will take Bill to drive 325 miles. How can you use the double number line to do this? _____

_____

_____

13 Describe how you can use the unit rate to find how long it will take Bill to drive 325 miles.

_____

14 How is solving a problem about constant speed similar to solving a problem about unit price? How are these types of problems different?

_____

_____

_____

_____

Try It

Use what you just learned about constant speed to solve these problems. Show your work on a separate sheet of paper.

15 A jet plane flew 1,200 miles in 3 hours. At that rate, how far will it travel in 2 hours?

_____

16 A small plane flew 240 miles in 2 hours. At that rate, how long will it take to travel 600 miles? _____

31

Read the problem below. Then explore different ways to solve problems involving converting measurement units.

> Toni is pouring milk for students' lunches. She knows that 3 quarts of milk contain 12 cups. How many cups can she pour with 7 quarts of milk? How many quarts does she need to pour 10 cups of milk?

Model It

You can use the unit rate to make a table.

The rate is 4 cups to 1 quart. The unit rate is 4.

Multiply each number of quarts by 4 to find the corresponding number of cups.

Quarts	1	2		4	5	6	7	8
Cups	4	8		16	20	24	28	32

The table shows that 7 quarts is the same as 28 cups of milk.

Model It

You can also use the unit rate to make a double number line. It's easy to see and use halfway points with a double number line.

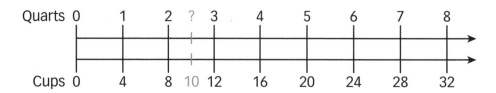

Locate 10 on the bottom number line. It is halfway between 8 and 12. This means that the number of quarts is halfway between 2 and 3 on the top number line, or $2\frac{1}{2}$ quarts.

Connect It

Now you will use the unit rate to solve the problem from the previous page.

17 Show how can you find the unit rate without using the models.

_____

18 Explain how you can use the unit rate to find the number of cups in 7 quarts.

_____

19 Explain how you can use the unit rate to find the number of quarts that is equal to 10 cups.

_____

_____

20 Compare the answers you computed in problems 17–19 to the models on the previous page. Describe the results.

_____

21 Now try a different problem. Given that there are 32 ounces in 2 pounds, explain how you would find the number of ounces in $4\frac{1}{2}$ pounds.

_____

_____

Try It

Use what you just learned about measurement units to solve these problems. Show your work on a separate sheet of paper.

22 Gary sees on a measuring cup that 200 centiliters are the same as 2 liters. How many liters are there in 300 centiliters? _____

23 When Gianna asks for 4 feet of ribbon, the clerk measures a 48-inch piece. How many inches long is a 9-foot piece of ribbon? _____

Study the model below. Then solve problems 24–26.

A hose fills an 18-gallon tub in 3 minutes. How long will it take to fill a 45-gallon tub?

Look at how you can solve the problem using the unit rate.

Ratio: 18 gallons to 3 minutes

Rate: 6 gallons for every 1 minute

Unit Rate: 6

45 gallons ÷ 6 = $7\frac{1}{2}$

Solution: ___$7\frac{1}{2}$ minutes___

The student used the information in the problem to find the unit rate. The unit rate can be used to find the time for any number of gallons.

💬 **Pair/Share**

How long would it take to fill a 90-gallon tub?

---

24 A store sells 4 ears of sweet corn for $1.00. How much will 9 ears cost?

Show your work.

How much does one ear of sweet corn cost?

💬 **Pair/Share**

Suppose you have $1.35 to spend. Why can't you spend that exact amount on corn?

Solution: _____

25 The male elephant at the city zoo weighs 8,000 pounds, which is the same as 4 tons. The female elephant weighs 7,000 pounds. How many tons does she weigh?

Show your work.

Does the number of tons have to be a whole number?

Solution: _____

◎ Pair/Share

Why do you know that the answer must be slightly less than 4?

26 Victor needs 30 feet of rope. The rope he wants to buy is sold by the yard. He knows that there are 3 feet in 1 yard. How many yards should he buy?

A 10

B 20

C 60

D 90

Natalia chose **D** as the correct answer. How did she get that answer?

_____

_____

_____

_____

Should the number of yards be less than or greater than the equivalent number of feet?

◎ Pair/Share

Why would the problem be more difficult if he needed to find the number of yards in 35 feet?

Solve the problems.

1 Cory knows that 16 tablespoons are the same as 1 cup. He needs to measure $\frac{3}{4}$ cup, but all he has is a tablespoon. How many tablespoons should Cory use?

A 4

B 8

C 12

D $21\frac{1}{3}$

2 Mrs. Rosso has to travel 390 miles on a highway. She drives 130 miles in 2 hours. If she has 7 hours to travel at that rate, will she arrive at her destination on time?

A Yes, she will arrive 1 hour early.

B Yes, she will arrive 4 hours early.

C No, she will arrive 1 hour late.

D No, she will arrive 4 hours late.

3 At Mark's Hardware, a package of 8 hinges costs $28. At Steve's Supplies, a package of 11 hinges costs $38. Which statement is the most accurate?

A Mark's Hardware is the better buy because it sells hinges at $3.50 per hinge.

B Mark's Hardware is the better buy because $28 is less than $38.

C Steve's Supplies is the better buy because it sells hinges at $3.45 per hinge.

D Steve's Supplies is the better buy because you get more hinges.

4 Elana can swim 12 laps in 4 minutes. Fill in the blanks in the double number line to show this relationship between laps and minutes.

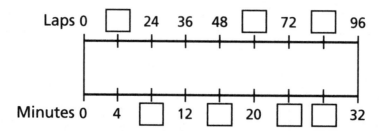

5 There are 4 cups in a quart and 4 quarts in a gallon. How many cups are in a 5-gallon jug of water?

Show your work.

Answer There are _____ cups in a 5-gallon jug of water.

6 Ivan and Jeff buy a package of 8 pens for $4.00. Ivan wants 5 of the pens, and Jeff wants 3. How much should each student pay?

Show your work.

Answer Ivan should pay _____ and Jeff should pay _____.

✓ **Self Check** *Go back and see what you can check off on the Self Check on page 1.*

L4: Solve Problems with Unit Rate

37

Lesson 5   Part 1: Introduction 👥
Solve Problems with Percent

CCSS
6.RP.A.3c

You have learned how to make tables of equivalent ratios to solve problems. Take a look at this problem.

> On the first math test, Keiko answered 19 out of 25 questions correctly. On the second test she got 17 out of 20 correct. On which test did she get a better grade?

🔍 Explore It

Use the math you already know to help solve the problem.

• Write a ratio in fraction form to compare the number correct to the total questions for each test. _____

• Can you compare these two ratios as they are written? Explain why or why not.

_____

_____

• Look at the table. How are 50, 75, and 100 related to 25?

_____

What do you need to do to complete the table? _____

Now complete the table.

Test 1	Number Correct	19			
	Total	25	50	75	100

• How are 40, 60, 80 and 100 related to 20?

_____

Use this information to complete a table of equivalent ratios for the second test.

• Look at the two tables. Which ratios can you use to compare the test results? Why?

Test 2	Number Correct	17				
	Total	20	40	60	80	100

_____

• On which test did Keiko get a better grade? Explain.

_____

_____

🔍 Find Out More

The ratios on the previous page, $\frac{76}{100}$ and $\frac{85}{100}$, can be expressed as fractions, decimals and percents. A **percent** is a rate "for every 100" or "per 100." The symbol % signifies percent.

Base-ten models can be used to represent fractions, decimals, and percents.

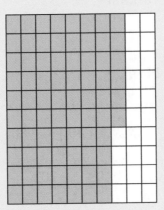   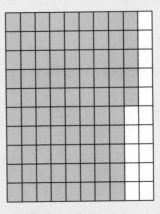

Fraction: $\frac{76}{100}$ Fraction: $\frac{85}{100}$

Decimal: 0.76   Decimal: 0.85

Percent: 76%   Percent: 85%

Here are some fractions, decimals, and percents that you will see and use often.

Fraction	$\frac{1}{100}$	$\frac{1}{10}$	$\frac{1}{4}$ or $\frac{25}{100}$	$\frac{1}{2}$ or $\frac{50}{100}$	$\frac{3}{4}$ or $\frac{75}{100}$	$\frac{1}{1}$ or $\frac{100}{100}$
Decimal	0.01	0.1 or 0.10	0.25	0.5 or 0.50	0.75	1.00
Percent	1%	10%	25%	50%	75%	100%

Sometimes it is easier to use an equivalent fraction when given a decimal or percent.

Example: What is 0.25 · 80?

Think: What is $\frac{1}{4}$ of 80? 80 ÷ 4 = 20

✏️ Reflect

1 Why do you think percents are used to compare ratios when the wholes are different?

_____

_____

Read the problem below. Then explore different ways to solve problems involving percent of a number.

> At Madison Middle School, 60% of the 800 students participate in music. How many students participate in music?

Picture It

You can use a bar model to solve the problem.

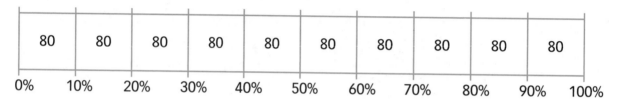

The bar model shows 800 students divided into 10 groups of 80. Each group of 80 represents 10%.

Model It

You can write an expression to find the number of students.

Use words:	60%	of	800
	⇓		⇓
Use numbers:	$\frac{60}{100}$	·	800

Remember: *of* means to multiply.

Connect It

Now you will solve the problem from the previous page using a bar model and related expression.

2 In the bar model, how many groups of 80 make up 60%? What is the total number of students in these groups?

_____

3 Using your answer to number 2, what is 60% of 800 students? _____

4 The expression from the previous page is shown below. Fill in the blanks to show how to multiply.

$$\frac{60}{100} \cdot \frac{800}{1} = \text{_____} \text{ or } \text{_____}$$

5 Explain how to find a percent of a number.

_____

_____

6 Imagine that 55% of the 800 students participate in music instead of 60%. How could you use the idea of halves with the bar model to find 55% of 800?

_____

_____

Try It

Use what you've just learned about the percent of a number to solve these problems. Show your work on a separate sheet of paper.

7 Charlie wants a new pair of shoes that cost $40. His mom pays 75% of the cost and Charlie pays 25%. How much do they each pay?

_____

8 A school will have a fall festival if at least 40% of the 500 students plan to attend. How many students must agree to attend in order for the school to have the festival?

_____

Read the problem below. Then explore different ways to find the whole when a part and the percent are given.

> Eric wants to buy a video game that costs $24, but he only wants to spend 40% of his savings. How much must Eric save in order to buy the game?

Picture It

You can use a double number line to find the whole when a part and the percent are given.

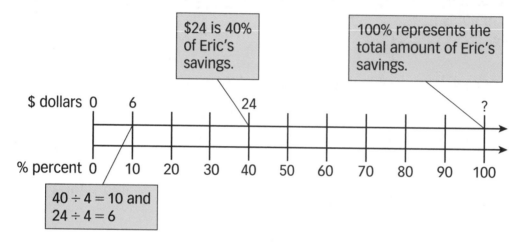

$24 is 40% of Eric's savings.

100% represents the total amount of Eric's savings.

$ dollars 0   6   24   ?

% percent 0   10   20   30   40   50   60   70   80   90   100

$40 \div 4 = 10$ and
$24 \div 4 = 6$

Model It

You can make a table of equivalent ratios to find the whole when a part and the percent are given.

$ dollars	6	12	24	?
% percent	10	20	40	100

Start with the ratio 24 to 40.

Find half of both quantities in 24 to 40: 12 to 20

Find half of both quantities in 12 to 20: 6 to 10

Connect It

Now you will solve the problem from the previous page using the double number line and the table.

9 Look at the table and the double number line. How many dollars is 10% of the total? _____ How many times greater than 10% is 100%? _____ So, how many times greater than $6 is the dollar amount that equals 100%? _____

10 Look at the double number line. Using the ratio 6 to 10, explain how you can find an equivalent ratio that has 100 as the second quantity.

_____

11 How much does Eric have to save in order to buy the game? _____

12 What does the answer to the problem mean? Fill in the blanks to help you understand.

10 • _____ = 100%   and   10 • $6 = $_____

If $24 is 40%, then $_____ is 100%.

So, 40% of $_____ is $24.

13 You can use what you know about finding percent of a number to check your answer. Fill in the blanks.

40% of $60

$\frac{40}{100} \cdot \frac{60}{1} =$ _____ or $_____

14 How can you find the whole when you know part and the percent?

_____

_____

_____

Try It

Use what you've just learned about finding the whole to solve this problem. Show your work on a separate sheet of paper.

15 150 students at York Middle School took part in the school clean up. This is 30% of the school's total students. How many students go to York Middle School? _____

Study the model below. Then solve problems 16–18.

If you find equivalent ratios with the denominator of 100, you can use percents.

Student Model

At Sydney's school, 300 of the 500 girls and 450 of the 600 boys attend the Spring Carnival. Which group has greater attendance?

Look at how you can use equivalent ratios and percents to solve the problem.

Girls	Boys
$\dfrac{300}{500} = \dfrac{60}{100}$	$\dfrac{450}{600} = \dfrac{75}{100}$
60%	75%

Solution: ___The boys have better attendance because 75% > 60%.___

Pair/Share

Why can't you say, "450 > 300, so the boys have better attendance?"

How can you use an equivalent ratios table to help you solve the problem?

16 Cesar turned in his third research report. His teacher said that Cesar had completed 20% of the reports for the school year. How many research reports will he do during the school year?

Show your work.

Pair/Share

Suppose you think of 20% as $\dfrac{20}{100}$ or $\dfrac{1}{5}$. How can you solve the problem using $\dfrac{1}{5}$ instead of 20%?

Solution: _____

17 Nia answered 80% of the 40 questions on a test correctly. How many correct answers did she have?

Show your work.

Solution: _____

When you write a number equation from a word equation, what symbol do you use for the word "of?"

💬**Pair/Share**

Did you use a fraction or a decimal to solve this problem? Why?

18 Andrei's grandfather offered to give him a gift of 50% of the amount of money he saved in one year. Andrei saved $120 dollars. How much did his grandfather give him as a gift?

A $50

B $60

C $120

D $180

Mitch chose **D** as the correct answer. How did he get that answer?

_____

_____

_____

_____

I think that it would be easy to solve this problem using a fraction.

💬**Pair/Share**

How can you show that your answer is 20% of 120?

Solve the problems.

1 Jason's father bought a computer for $800. He made equal payments of 25% of the total cost. How much was each payment?

A $25

B $32

C $200

D $400

2 Antonio has read 147 pages of a book. He has completed 70% of the book. How many more pages does he need to read to finish the book?

☐ pages

3 During the basketball season, Cory made 21 of the 60 baskets she attempted. Krista made 18 of the 45 baskets she attempted. Paula made 17 of the 50 baskets she attempted. Write the names of the players in order from the lowest percentage of baskets made to the highest percentage of baskets made.

Lowest ──────────────────→ Highest

NAME	NAME	NAME

4 Jackson's mom limits the amount of time he is allowed to play video games. After Jackson plays for 9 minutes, his mom tells him that he has used up 30% of his time. How many more minutes can Jackson play before he uses all of his time?

Show your work.

Answer Jackson can play _____ more minutes.

5 Ashley has sold 70% of the 20 candy bars she is supposed to sell for her softball team. How many candy bars does she have left to sell?

Show your work.

Answer Ashley has _____ more candy bars to sell.

 **Self Check** *Go back and see what you can check off on the Self Check on page 1.*

Solve the problems.

1 A pottery maker can make 24 vases in 8 days. If the pottery maker works 6 hours each day, how long does it take to make 1 vase?

A 2 hours

B 3 hours

C 4 hours

D 6 hours

2 A carpenter needs to make 60 dowels. Each dowel must be 6 inches long. The wood from which the carpenter will cut the dowels comes in 4-foot lengths. What is the *least* number of 4-foot lengths of wood the carpenter can buy and still make all 60 dowels?

A 6

B 7

C 8

D 9

3 One batch of vegetable soup uses 2 cups of chopped onions, 1.5 cups of chopped celery, and 1 cup of chopped carrots. Select each ratio that will help a chef compare cups of chopped carrots to total cups of chopped vegetables. Circle all that apply.

A 2 to 7   D 4 to 18

B 2 to 9   E 9 to 2

C 4 to 9

4 A company sells crushed rock in 16-pound bags, each bag containing a mixture of quartz and marble. The table below lists the amounts of quartz and marble needed to fill a certain number of bags. If the ratio of quartz to marble is the same for every bag, fill in the empty cells to complete the table.

BAGS OF ROCK

Number of Bags	Quartz (pounds)	Marble (pounds)
3	27	21
8	☐	56
☐	99	☐
14	☐	98
☐	135	☐

5   A bookstore is having a sale in which you can get 4 notebooks for $7.00 and 10 folders for $2.50. How much will it cost Rico to buy 5 notebooks and 6 folders?

Show your work.

Answer _____

6   Shoe store A is having a sale in which every pair of shoes is 40% off the regular price. Shoe store B is having a sale in which $40 is deducted from the regular price.

Part A

Richard is comparing the price of the same pair of shoes in both stores. In both stores, the shoes normally sell for $120. Which store has the better bargain?

Show your work.

Answer _____

Part B

Gwen buys 3 identical pairs of shoes at Store A. She pays $110.25 after the discount. What is the regular price of each pair?

Show your work.

Answer _____

Performance Task

Answer the questions and show all your work on separate paper.

A local snack food company asks you to develop a healthy trail mix recipe. They will sell the trail mix in a 6-serving package. The company gives you a list of requirements.

- The ratio of weight of fruits to weight of nuts and/or seeds must be 2 : 1.

- The trail mix must have 4 or more ingredients.

- One serving must be between 1 and 2 ounces.

- The cost per serving must be between $0.35 and $0.50.

Develop your recipe and include the total weight and cost for 1 serving. Then write your recipe for 6 servings and include the total weight and cost for this amount. Explain how your recipe meets all the requirements.

☑ CHECKLIST
Did you . . .
☐ Find the costs per ounce?
☐ Meet all the requirements?
☐ Check all your calculations?

Ingredient	Cost per pound
Nuts and Seeds	
Peanuts	$3.99
Almonds	$7.99
Sunflower seeds	$2.99
Fruits	
Dried banana chips	$3.49
Dried cranberries	$4.99
Raisins	$4.99

Reflect on Mathematical Practices

After you complete the task, choose one of the following questions to answer.

1. **Persevere** What was your plan for solving the problem?

2. **Be Precise** How did you make sure you met all the requirements?

Unit 2
The Number System

There are many situations in your life where you will need only a portion of something. You might need to divide a pizza into 8 pieces. You might need to use only half of an 8.5 meter piece of rope. Or you might find the perfect recipe for chocolate fudge calls for $4\frac{3}{4}$ pounds of chocolate, but you only have $\frac{1}{2}$ pound of chocolate. In all of these situations—whether the numbers are whole numbers, fractions, or decimals— understanding the numbers and how to divide them is important to solving your problem. In this unit, you will come to understand many different kinds of numbers and how they relate to each other.

✓ Self Check

Before starting this unit, check off the skills you know below. As you complete each lesson, see how many more you can check off!

I can:	Before this unit	After this unit
explain how to divide fractions, for example: explain why $\frac{2}{3} \div \frac{3}{4} = \frac{8}{9}$	☐	☐
divide multi-digit whole numbers, for example: $26{,}304 \div 24 = 1{,}096$	☐	☐
add and subtract multi-digit decimals, for example: $3.1 - 1.534 = 1.566$	☐	☐
multiply and divide decimals, for example: $32.5 \div 0.25 = 130$	☐	☐
find common factors and common multiples, for example: common factors of 4 and 6 are 1 and 2, and common multiples are 12 and 24.	☐	☐
recognize real-world uses for negative numbers and locate them on a number line	☐	☐
order integers and find absolute value, for example: $^-7 < ^-5$ and $^-5 < 2$	☐	☐
plot points in 4 quadrants of the coordinate plane	☐	☐

Lesson 6 Part 1: Introduction

Understand Division with Fractions

What does it mean to divide a fraction by a fraction?

You know how to divide a whole number by a unit fraction. For example, you can think of 6 divided by $\frac{1}{4}$ as "how many one-fourths are there in 6?" Using a number line, you can divide 6 into fourths and count to see there are 24 fourths in 6.

$$6 \div \frac{1}{4} = 24$$

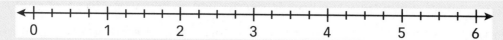

You also learned that dividing a number by a fraction is the same as multiplying the number by the reciprocal of the fraction.

$6 \div \frac{1}{4}$ is the same as 6×4, or 24

🔍 **Think** What does dividing a whole number by a fraction mean?

Madison cuts a 6-yard length of ribbon into $\frac{3}{4}$ yard pieces.

To figure out how many pieces Madison cut, think, "How many three-fourths are in 6?"

You can draw the same number line to represent the 6 yards of ribbon and divide it into fourths.

> **Circle the multiplication expression that is the same as the division expression.**

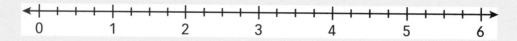

You can circle three $\frac{1}{4}$ sections to represent $\frac{3}{4}$ yard pieces. You can see there are eight $\frac{3}{4}$ yard pieces in 6 yards.

$$6 \div \frac{3}{4} = 8$$

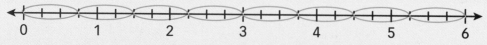

$$6 \times \frac{4}{3} = 8$$

🔍 **Think**   What does dividing a fraction by a whole number mean?

Cory wants to pour $\frac{3}{4}$ of a quart of juice equally into 6 glasses. This means he needs to divide $\frac{3}{4}$ into 6 equal parts. You can represent the problem with an area model. First, you can show the $\frac{3}{4}$ quart of juice. Then, you can draw vertical lines to divide the model into 6 equal parts.

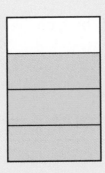 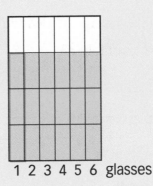

1 2 3 4 5 6 glasses

$$\frac{3}{4} \div 6 = \frac{3}{24} = \frac{1}{8}$$

$\frac{3}{4}$ quart of juice divided equally into 6 glasses means Cory will pour $\frac{3}{24}$ or $\frac{1}{8}$ quart of juice into each glass.

$\frac{3}{4} \div 6$ is the same as $\frac{3}{4} \times \frac{1}{6}$.

Cory pours $\frac{1}{6}$ of $\frac{3}{4}$ quart of juice into each glass.

✏️ **Reflect**

1 Use the number line to show and explain why $\frac{4}{10} \div 2$ and $\frac{4}{10} \times \frac{1}{2}$ both equal $\frac{2}{10}$.

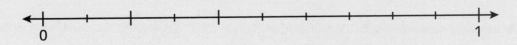

0   1

_____

_____

_____

Explore It

Explore dividing a fraction by a fraction with the problem below.

Kate has $\frac{2}{3}$ yards of fabric to make small flags. Each flag requires $\frac{1}{6}$ yard of fabric. How many flags can Kate make?

2 You need to find out how many _____ are in _____.

3 The number lines below are divided into thirds. Label $\frac{2}{3}$ on the top number line to represent $\frac{2}{3}$ yards of fabric.

4 Each flag requires $\frac{1}{6}$ yard of fabric. Divide the bottom number line into sixths to show how many sixths are in $\frac{2}{3}$.

5 Look at the bottom number line. How many sixths are there in $\frac{2}{3}$? _____

6 How many flags can Kate make? _____

7 $\frac{2}{3} \div \frac{1}{6} =$ _____

8 $\frac{2}{3} \times$ _____ $= 4$

Talk About It

Solve the problem below as a group.

Kevin has 6 cups of flour. It takes $\frac{3}{8}$ cup of flour to make one cake. How many cakes can Kevin make?

9 You need to find out how many _____ are in _____ .

10 Do you think the number of cakes Kevin can make is greater than or less than 6? Why?

_____

11 Represent 6 cups with 6 rectangles. 4 rectangles are shown below. Draw 2 more rectangles.

12 Circle and count groups of $\frac{3}{8}$ in the model. How many did you circle? _____

13 How many $\frac{3}{8}$-cups of flour are in 6 cups of flour? _____

14 $6 \div \frac{3}{8} =$ _____

✎ **Try It Another Way**

Explore dividing by a unit fraction using a common denominator.

To solve $5 \div \frac{1}{2}$, write 5 as a fraction with a denominator of 2 and think, "How many halves are in ten halves?" $\frac{10}{2} \div \frac{1}{2} = 10$. Use the same reasoning to find $\frac{8}{6} \div \frac{2}{3}$.

15 Write $\frac{8}{6}$ as a fraction with a denominator of 3. _____ To solve $\frac{4}{3} \div \frac{2}{3}$, think, "How many two-thirds are in four-thirds"? _____

16 Write $\frac{2}{3}$ as a fraction with a denominator of 6. _____ To solve $\frac{8}{6} \div \frac{4}{6}$, think, "How many four-sixths are in eight-sixths"? _____

Connect It

Talk through these problems as a class, then write your answers below.

17 **Explain:** Look at the model below. Write the division equation that the model represents. Explain how to find the quotient using the model.

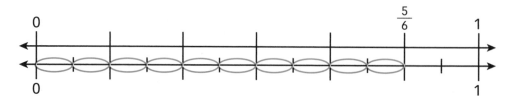

_____

_____

18 **Analyze:** Sam said that $\frac{3}{2} \div \frac{1}{4}$ equals $\frac{3}{8}$. Draw a model and use words to explain why Sam's statement is not reasonable.

_____

_____

_____

_____

19 **Justify:** Show that $2 \div \frac{4}{6} = 3$ by using a model. Explain why the answer is greater than the number you started with.

_____

_____

Put It Together

20 Use what you have learned to complete this task.

Choose one of the following problems to solve. Circle the problem you choose.

Greg made $\frac{2}{3}$ gallon of lemonade and plans to share it equally among 4 friends. How much lemonade will each friend get?

Keisha plans to run 4 miles this week. If she runs $\frac{2}{3}$ of a mile each day, how many days will it take her to run 4 miles? Will she be able to run 4 miles in a week?

A Write a division expression and draw a model to represent the problem.

_____

_____

_____

B Estimate what you think the quotient will be. Will the quotient be greater than or less than the dividend? How do you know?

_____

_____

_____

_____

_____

_____

C Use your model to explain how to find the quotient and what the quotient means.

_____

_____

_____

_____

Lesson 7   Part 1: Introduction 👥

Divide with Fractions

In the previous lesson, you learned what dividing by fractions means. In this lesson you will divide with fractions to solve problems. Take a look at this problem.

Charlie is growing vegetables in planters. He has 4 bags of soil and uses $\frac{2}{3}$ of a bag of soil to fill each planter. How many planters can he fill?

🔍 Explore It

Use the math you already know to solve the problem.

● Think of the number of planters that Charlie can fill as how many $\frac{2}{3}$s are in 4. Will that number be greater than or less than 4? Explain your reasoning.

_____

_____

● The model below represents the 4 bags of soil. Draw horizontal lines to divide each bag into thirds.

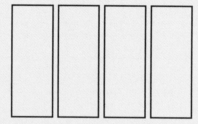

● Circle and count groups of $\frac{2}{3}$ in the model. How many did you circle? _____

● Why do you circle groups of $\frac{2}{3}$ to represent this problem?

_____

_____

● How many planters can Charlie fill? _____

● Explain how the model helped you solve the problem.

_____

_____

Find Out More

When you found the number of $\frac{2}{3}$ s that are in 4, you were dividing. You are solving the problem $4 \div \frac{2}{3}$. You can solve this problem by multiplying.

You know that multiplication and division are related. 4 divided by 2 is the same as $\frac{1}{2}$ of 4, or multiplying 4 by $\frac{1}{2}$.

$$4 \div 2 = 2$$

$$4 \times \frac{1}{2} = 2$$

> Think of 2 as $\frac{2}{1}$. Dividing by $\frac{2}{1}$ is the same as multiplying by $\frac{1}{2}$.

When dividing with unit fractions, you learned that dividing 4 by $\frac{1}{3}$ is the same as multiplying 4 by 3.

$$4 \div \frac{1}{3} = 12$$

$$4 \times 3 = 12$$

> Dividing by $\frac{1}{3}$ is the same as multiplying by $\frac{3}{1}$ or 3.

Dividing with any fraction works the same way. Dividing 4 by $\frac{2}{3}$ is the same as multiplying 4 by $\frac{3}{2}$.

$$4 \div \frac{2}{3} = 6$$

$$4 \times \frac{3}{2} = \frac{12}{2}$$

$$= 6$$

> Dividing by $\frac{2}{3}$ is the same as multiplying by $\frac{3}{2}$.

You can solve any division problem using multiplication. To divide by any number, you can multiply by its **multiplicative inverse**, which is also known as the **reciprocal**.

Reflect

1 Explain how you can solve this division problem by using multiplication.

$6 \div \frac{2}{3}$

_____

_____

_____

Read the problem below. Then explore how to divide a whole number by a fraction.

Kelly drank $\frac{2}{5}$ of the water in her bottle. She drank 3 cups of water. How many total cups of water were in her bottle?

Picture It

You can draw a picture to understand the problem.

The bar represents Kelly's water bottle. You can divide the bar into fifths and shade $\frac{2}{5}$ to represent the amount of water Kelly drank, 3 cups.

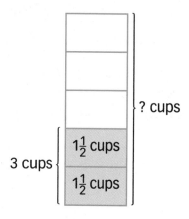

Model It

You can use words and equations to understand the problem.

$\frac{2}{5}$ of the total amount of water equals 3.

$\frac{2}{5}$	of	the total amount of water	equals	3
$\frac{2}{5}$	$\times$	?	=	3

To solve a missing factor problem like $\frac{2}{5} \times ? = 3$, you can divide.

$? = 3 \div \frac{2}{5}$

Connect It

Now you will solve the problem from the previous page using the picture and model.

2 Look at Picture It on the previous page. Why do you divide the bar into fifths?

_____

3 How can you use Picture It to find out how many cups of water are in the bottle?

_____

_____

4 How many total cups of water were in Kelly's bottle?

_____

5 Look at Model It on the previous page. Find $3 \div \frac{2}{5}$. Show your work.

_____

6 Explain how to use multiplication to divide a whole number by a fraction.

_____

_____

Try It

Use what you just learned about dividing with fractions to solve these problems. Show your work on a separate sheet of paper.

7 How many $1\frac{1}{2}$-cup servings are there in 12 cups of juice? _____

8 It takes Emily 9 minutes to bicycle $\frac{3}{10}$ of the way to school. How many minutes does it take Emily to bicycle all the way to school? _____

Read the problem below. Then explore how to divide a fraction by a fraction.

> Eli ran $\frac{3}{4}$ of a mile. Every $\frac{1}{8}$ of a mile, he jumped over a hurdle. There was a final hurdle at the $\frac{3}{4}$ mile mark. How many hurdles did Eli jump over?

🔍 Picture It

You can draw a picture to understand the problem.

The top number line shows the distance Eli ran, $\frac{3}{4}$ mile.

The bottom number line shows the number of $\frac{1}{8}$s that are in $\frac{3}{4}$.

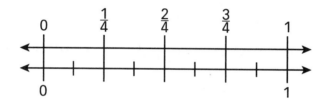

🔍 Model It

You can use words and equations to understand the problem.

Think: How many $\frac{1}{8}$s are in $\frac{3}{4}$?

Use division to find how many $\frac{1}{8}$s are in $\frac{3}{4}$.

$\frac{3}{4}$	divided into	$\frac{1}{8}$s	equals	the number of hurdles
$\frac{3}{4}$	$\div$	$\frac{1}{8}$	$=$	?

$\frac{3}{4} \div \frac{1}{8} = ?$

Connect It

Now you will solve the problem from the previous page using the picture and model.

9 Look at Picture It. Why is the top number line divided into fourths? Why is the bottom number line divided into eighths?

_____

_____

_____

10 Explain how Picture It helps you figure out how many hurdles Eli jumped over.

_____

11 How many hurdles did Eli jump over? _____

12 Look at Model It. Explain how to use multiplication to find $\frac{3}{4} \div \frac{1}{8}$.

_____

_____

13 Evaluate $\frac{3}{4} \div \frac{1}{8}$. Show your work. _____

14 Explain how to divide a fraction by a fraction.

_____

_____

Try It

Use what you just learned to solve these problems. Show your work on a separate sheet of paper.

15 Keisha cuts a $\frac{2}{3}$-foot rope into $\frac{1}{12}$-foot pieces. How many pieces of rope did

she cut? _____

16 Jade makes half a liter of lemonade. She pours $\frac{1}{10}$ liter of lemonade into each glass.

How many glasses is Jade able to fill? _____

Read the problem below. Then explore how to divide a mixed number by a fraction.

> Mari divides $1\frac{4}{5}$ pounds of granola into $\frac{2}{5}$-pound bags for a bake sale. How many bags of granola can she sell?

🔍 Picture It

You can draw a picture to understand the problem.

The shaded bars represent $1\frac{4}{5}$ pounds of granola.

Each circle shows a $\frac{2}{5}$-pound bag of granola.

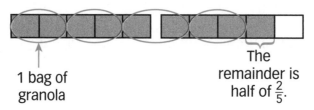

1 bag of granola

The remainder is half of $\frac{2}{5}$.

🔍 Model It

You can use words and equations to understand the problem.

Think: How many $\frac{2}{5}$s are in $1\frac{4}{5}$?

Use division to find how many $\frac{2}{5}$s are in $1\frac{4}{5}$.

$1\frac{4}{5}$	divided into	$\frac{2}{5}$s	equals	the number of bags of granola
$1\frac{4}{5}$	÷	$\frac{2}{5}$	=	?

$$1\frac{4}{5} \div \frac{2}{5} = ?$$

$$\frac{9}{5} \div \frac{2}{5} = ?$$

Connect It

Now you will solve the problem from the previous page using the picture and model.

17 Look at Picture It. Why do you circle groups of $\frac{2}{5}$ to solve this problem?

_____

_____

18 Count the circles. How many $\frac{2}{5}$-pound bags of granola can Mari sell? _____

19 What fraction of a bag would the remaining $\frac{1}{5}$ pound of granola be? Explain your answer.

_____

_____

20 Look at the Model It. Explain how you know $1\frac{4}{5}$ is equal to $\frac{9}{5}$.

_____

21 Explain how to use multiplication to evaluate $\frac{9}{5} \div \frac{2}{5}$.

_____

_____

22 Evaluate $\frac{9}{5} \div \frac{2}{5}$. Show your work. _____

23 Explain how to divide with mixed numbers.

_____

_____

Try It

Use what you just learned to solve these problems. Show your work on a separate sheet of paper.

24 A recipe requires $\frac{3}{4}$ of a cup of water. Kyle has a $1\frac{1}{2}$-cup measuring cup. How much of the measuring cup is filled with water? _____

25 How many $\frac{1}{3}$-cup servings are in $\frac{5}{6}$ cup? _____

Study the student model below. Then solve problems 26–28.

> Student Model

The student divided the number of gallons of paint used, $1\frac{1}{2}$, by the gallons of paint she bought, $2\frac{1}{2}$.

Lydia bought $2\frac{1}{2}$ gallons of paint and used $1\frac{1}{2}$ gallons of paint. What fraction of the paint did she use?

Look at how you can show your work using a model.

Think: What fraction of $2\frac{1}{2}$ is $1\frac{1}{2}$?

Some fraction of $2\frac{1}{2}$ equals $1\frac{1}{2}$.

$$? \quad \times 2\frac{1}{2} \quad = \quad 1\frac{1}{2}$$

To solve $? \times 2\frac{1}{2} = 1\frac{1}{2}$, divide.

$$? = 1\frac{1}{2} \div 2\frac{1}{2}$$

$$= \frac{3}{2} \div \frac{5}{2}$$

$$\frac{3}{2} \div \frac{5}{2} = \frac{3}{2} \times \frac{2}{5}; \frac{3}{2} \times \frac{2}{5} = \frac{6}{10} \text{ or } \frac{3}{5}$$

Solution: Lydia used $\frac{3}{5}$ of the paint she bought.

💬 Pair/Share

How could you justify your answer with a picture?

💬 Pair/Share

How did you and your partner decide which fraction is the dividend and which is the divisor?

Will the answer be less than 1 or greater than 1? Why?

26 Lexi has planted seeds in $\frac{3}{5}$ of the garden. She used $\frac{1}{2}$ pound of seeds. How many pounds will she use for the entire garden?

Show your work.

Solution: _____

27 A marathon is $\frac{131}{5}$ miles long. If 4 people divide up the distance equally, how many miles does each person need to run?

Show your work.

Dividing by 4 is the same as multiplying by what number?

◯Pair/Share

How is this problem different from the others you've seen in this lesson?

Solution: _____

28 Which of the following problems can be solved by finding $4 \div \frac{2}{3}$?

A 4 people equally share $\frac{2}{3}$ of a pizza. How much of the pizza does each person eat?

B How many $\frac{2}{3}$-cup servings of soup are in 4 cups of soup?

C A pie recipe requires $\frac{2}{3}$ pounds of apples. How many apples are needed for 4 pies?

D A family ate $\frac{2}{3}$ of a 4-foot sandwich. How much did they eat?

Arthur chose **A** as the correct answer. How did he get that answer?

_____

_____

_____

_____

What kind of picture could represent the expression?

◯Pair/Share

Does Arthur's answer make sense?

Solve the problems.

1 What is the value of the expression $\frac{3}{8} \div 1\frac{1}{2}$?

A $\frac{9}{16}$

B $\frac{6}{8}$

C 4

D $\frac{1}{4}$

2 Find the expression that does NOT answer the question: "What fraction of 8 is $2\frac{1}{2}$?"

A $2\frac{1}{2} \div 8$

B $\frac{5}{2} \times \frac{1}{8}$

C $8 \div 2\frac{1}{2}$

D $? \times 8 = 2\frac{1}{2}$

3 The area and one dimension of a piece of land are given. From the list, write the fraction inside each box that represents the second dimension of the piece of land described.

$\frac{3}{7}$	$\frac{7}{8}$	☐	The area of a rectangular piece of land is $\frac{1}{2}$ square mile. One dimension of this piece of land is $\frac{7}{8}$ mile.
$\frac{4}{7}$	$\frac{4}{9}$	☐	The area of a piece of land that is in the shape of a triangle is $\frac{1}{12}$ square mile. One dimension of this piece of land is $\frac{4}{21}$ mile.
$\frac{5}{7}$	$\frac{5}{9}$		
$\frac{5}{8}$	$\frac{7}{9}$	☐	The area of a rectangular piece of land is $\frac{2}{3}$ square mile. One dimension is $1\frac{1}{2}$ miles.

4 Write each expression in the correct column to show whether the quotient is less than, greater than, or equal to 1.

$\frac{3}{4} \div \frac{1}{2}$ $\frac{1}{2} \div \frac{3}{4}$ $\frac{2}{9} \div \frac{1}{27}$ $\frac{5}{3} \div \frac{20}{6}$ $\frac{4}{3} \div \frac{3}{5}$ $\frac{19}{8} \div 2\frac{3}{8}$	quotient is less than 1	quotient is equal to 1	quotient is greater than 1

5 Explain the difference between dividing in half and dividing by half using pictures, models, or numbers.

_____

_____

_____

_____

6 Write a story to represent the expression $6 \div \frac{3}{4}$. Draw a model and use multiplication to show the solution. Explain how the dividend, divisor, and quotient relate to the story.

_____

_____

_____

_____

_____

_____

 **Self Check** *Go back and see what you can check off on the Self Check on page 51.*

Lesson 8   Part 1: Introduction 👥

Divide Multi-Digit Numbers

CCSS
6.NS.B.2

In 5th grade, you learned how to divide using models and partial quotients. Take a look at this problem.

> For a fundraiser, the sixth graders have 288 bags of popcorn to sell. There are 3 sixth-grade classes. If each class sells an equal number of bags, how many bags of popcorn does each class sell?

🔍 Explore It

Use the math you already know to solve the problem.

▪ Use a bar model to represent the problem. Fill in the whole and the number of groups.

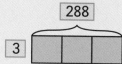

▪ What division expression represents this problem? _____

▪ Estimate the quotient. The quotient is around _____ . Explain your thinking.

_____

▪ Use your estimate. At least how many bags of popcorn should each class sell? _____

▪ How many bags are left to sell altogether? _____ By each class? _____

▪ How many more bags can each class sell? How do you know?

_____

▪ Explain how to find the total number of bags of popcorn each class can sell.

_____

_____

Find Out More

You used partial quotients to solve the problem.

$$
\begin{array}{r}
96 \leftarrow \text{quotient} \\
6 \left.\vphantom{\begin{array}{c}6\\90\end{array}}\right\} \text{partial quotients} \\
90 \\
\text{divisor} \rightarrow 3\,\overline{)288} \leftarrow \text{dividend} \\
270 \leftarrow 90 \times 3 \\
\overline{18} \\
18 \leftarrow 6 \times 3 \\
\overline{0}
\end{array}
$$

You know that 90 groups of 3 is 270.
Subtract to find how many are left.
$288 - 270 = 18$

You know 6 equal groups of 3 is 18.
Subtract to find how many are left. $18 - 18 = 0$

To find the quotient, add the partial quotients.
$90 + 6 = 96$. So, $288 \div 3 = 96$.

You can also use the division algorithm to find the quotient.
This method is like partial quotients, except you need to pay attention to place value.

You know the quotient is around 90.

$$
\begin{array}{r}
\text{H T O} \\
96 \\
3\,\overline{)288} \\
270 \leftarrow 27 \text{ tens or } 270 \text{ ones} \\
\overline{18} \leftarrow 18 \text{ ones} \\
18 \\
\overline{0}
\end{array}
$$

288 is 28 tens and 8 ones.
There are 9 groups of 3 in 28.
9 tens $\times$ 3 ones = 27 tens.
28 tens $-$ 27 tens = 1 ten

27 tens is the same as 270 ones.
When you bring down the 8 ones to get 18,
you are subtracting 270 from 288.

There are 6 groups of 3 in 18.
6 ones $\times$ 3 = 18 ones.
18 ones $-$ 18 ones = 0. There is no remainder.

So, $288 \div 3 = 96$.

Reflect

1. To divide 343 by 9, would you use partial quotients or the division algorithm? Explain your reasoning.

_____

_____

_____

Read the problem below. Then explore how to divide with a two-digit divisor using partial quotients or the division algorithm.

A family is heading out on a car trip of 672 miles to what is known as the sixth most popular National Park, the Blue Ridge Parkway. If they travel at an average of 56 miles per hour, how long will it take to get there?

Estimate It

You can use compatible numbers to estimate the quotient.

$660 \div 60 = 11$

Model It

You can use partial quotients to divide.

```
                    12 ← quotient
                     2 ⎤
                    10 ⎦ partial quotients
divisor → 56 ) 672 ← dividend
               560 ← 10 × 56
               112
               112 ← 2 × 56
                 0
```

Model It

You can use the division algorithm to divide.

```
        H T O
          1 2
   56 ) 6 7 2
        5 6↓   ← 56 tens
        1 1 2  ← 112 ones
        1 1 2
            0
```

672 is 67 tens and 2 ones.
There is 1 group of 56 in 67.
1 ten × 56 = 56 tens
67 tens − 56 tens = 11 tens

Bring down the 2.

There are 2 groups of 56 in 112.
2 ones × 56 = 112 ones
112 ones − 112 ones = 0 ones

Connect It

Now compare the two methods of dividing to solve the problem.

2 Why does it make sense to use 660 and 60 to estimate the quotient?

_____

3 How is writing the 1 in the division algorithm the same as writing the 10 in the partial

quotients model? _____

4 How is writing the 56 in the division algorithm the same as writing the 560 in the

partial quotients model? _____

_____

5 When solving this problem with the division algorithm, how is bringing down the
2 ones like the first subtraction step in the partial quotients method?

_____

_____

6 How long will it take the family to drive to the park? _____ How can you check

your answer? _____

7 How is using the division algorithm to divide the same as using partial quotients to

divide? How is it different? _____

_____

Try It

**Use what you just learned about dividing to solve these problems. Show your
work on a separate sheet of paper.**

8 A grandmother has $490 that she wants to give to her 14 grandchildren. How much

money will each grandchild receive if they each receive an equal amount? _____

9 18 students collected cans for a school recycling project. If the students collected a

total of 306 cans, how many cans did each student collect? _____

Read the problem below. Then explore how to divide a 5-digit dividend by a 2-digit divisor.

> Sam's father bought a new car for $26,304. He expects to pay for it in 24 equal monthly payments. How much will Sam's father have to pay each month?

Estimate It

You can use compatible numbers to estimate the solution.

$24,000 ÷ 24 = $1,000

Model It

You can use the division algorithm to solve the problem.

```
       Th H T O
        1096
  24) 26,304
      24↓
      23
       0↓
      230
      216↓
      144
      144
        0
```

26,304 is 26 thousands, 3 hundreds, and 4 ones.

There is 1 group of 24 in 26.
1 thousand × 24 = 24 thousands
26 thousands − 24 thousands = 2 thousands
Bring down the 3.

There are no groups of 24 in 23.
0 hundreds × 24 = 0 hundreds
23 hundreds − 0 hundreds = 23 hundreds
Bring down the 0.

There are 9 groups of 24 in 230.
9 tens × 24 = 216 tens
230 tens − 216 tens = 14 tens
Bring down the 4.

There are 6 groups of 24 in 144.
6 ones × 24 = 144 ones
144 ones − 144 ones = 0 ones
There is no remainder.

Connect It

Now answer the question and think about the division algorithm.

10 How much will Sam's father have to pay each month? _____ Is that answer

reasonable? Explain. _____

11 Look back at the division algorithm. What is 24 × $1,096? _____

12 Suppose Sam's father decides to pay for the car in 48 monthly payments. How much

would he have to pay each month?_____

Show your work.

13 Why is it important to pay close attention to place value when dividing with the

division algorithm? _____

_____

Try It

Use what you just learned to solve these problems. Show your work on a separate sheet of paper.

14 In a year (12 months), a sports team practiced for a total of 1,305 hours. On average, how many hours did the team practice each month?

_____

15 There are 1,891 students participating in the citywide holiday concert. A bus seats 62 students. How many buses will be needed to bring the students to the concert?

_____

_____

Study the student model below. Then solve problems 16–18.

> *The student remembered to write a 0 in the ones place in the quotient to show that there were no ones left.*

◯Pair/Share

How could you check your answer?

Student Model

The marching band packed 3,060 cans of juice into boxes for a band competition. Each box holds 18 cans. How many boxes did the band members have to carry?

Look at how you could show your work using the division algorithm.

$$
\begin{array}{r}
170 \\
18\overline{)3{,}060} \\
-18 \\
\hline
126 \\
-126 \\
\hline
0 \\
\end{array}
$$

Solution: ___170 boxes___

> *What is a good estimate for the quotient?*

◯Pair/Share

Does your answer make sense?

16 A local bank donated 4,074 pencils to distribute to the 42 sixth-grade classes in the district. How many pencils did each class receive?

Show your work.

Solution: _____

17 At an amusement park, only 18 people are allowed on a ride at the same time. There are 157 people waiting in line. How many groups will there be?

Show your work.

If there is a remainder, I need to decide whether to round up or down.

Solution: _____

💬**Pair/Share**

Compare the steps you each took to solve this problem.

18 Route 80 runs a little over 2,900 miles across the United States from the New York City area to San Francisco. If you drove the entire length in 14 days, on average how many miles would you travel per day? Circle the correct answer.

A a little more than 27 miles per day

B a little more than 2,070 miles per day

C a little more than 207 miles per day

D a little more than $\frac{27}{10}$ miles per day

Cody chose **A** as the correct answer. How did he get that answer?

What is the whole in this problem?

_____

_____

_____

_____

💬**Pair/Share**

Talk about the problem and explain how you could get each of the answers.

Solve the problems.

1 Charlotte read a 608-page book in 16 hours last month. How many pages per hour was that?

A   38 pages

B   380 pages

C $4\frac{2}{16}$ pages

D   3 R4 pages

2 There are 3,072 books in the school library. There are 96 sixth graders. If the sixth graders teamed up to read all the books, how many books would each sixth grader need to read?

A   about 4 books

B   32 books

C $30\frac{72}{100}$ books

D   about 307 books

3 A farmer needs to pack 2,903 apples into crates to ship to supermarkets. Each crate can hold only 30 apples. Choose True or False for each statement.

A   The farmer needs 96 crates to ship out all the apples.   ☐ True   ☐ False

B   The farmer needs 97 crates to ship out all the apples.   ☐ True   ☐ False

C   At least one of the crates will not be filled to capacity.   ☐ True   ☐ False

D   To determine the number of crates needed, divide 2,903 by 30.   ☐ True   ☐ False

4 In each box, write the appropriate digit to complete the division algorithm.

$$
\begin{array}{r}
9\ \square \\
2\,5\,6\,)\overline{2\ \square\ 8\ 3\ 5} \\
-\ 2\,3\,0\,4 \\
\hline
1\ 7\ 9\ \square \\
-\ 1\,7\,9\,2 \\
\hline
\square
\end{array}
$$

5 An elementary school received a donation of $1,000. The school has 4 kindergarten classes and 3 classes each in Grades 1 through 6. Can the money be divided equally among the classes? Explain.

Show your work.

Answer _____

_____

6 The seating capacity of a basketball stadium is 5,782. The seats are arranged in 24 sections of the same size. Any seats that are left over from the 24 sections are called "priority seating." How many seats are called "priority seating"?

Show your work.

Answer _____

 ✓ **Self Check** *Go back and see what you can check off on the Self Check on page 51.*

Lesson 9　Part 1: Introduction 👥

Add and Subtract Decimals

CCSS
6.NS.B.3

You've learned what decimals are and how to add and subtract them to tenths and hundredths. Take a look at this problem.

Zee wants to make 2 liters of pink lemonade for a party. She squeezed the eight lemons she had and got 0.375 liters of lemon juice. She had 0.35 liters of cranberry juice, and 1.2 liters of water.

How much lemonade can she make? How much more or less than 2 liters will she have?

🔍 Explore It

Use the math you know to answer the question.

⬤ How can you estimate the amount?

_____

_____

⬤ How can you read each amount in words?

_____

⬤ How can you convert these different amounts to thousandths?

_____

_____

⬤ How can you write the equation to make sure the place values line up?

_____

⬤ Write the sum of the total amount of lemonade. _____

⬤ How can you find the difference between that number and 2 liters?

_____

Find Out More

You can see that what you know about adding and subtracting whole numbers can help you add and subtract decimals to the thousandths.

The important thing is that you have to make sure you are adding the same place values. You can use a place-value chart to help you keep your columns lined up.

Ones	.	Tenths $\frac{1}{10}$	Hundredths $\frac{1}{100}$	Thousandths $\frac{1}{1,000}$
0	.	3	7	5
+0	.	3	5	0
+1	.	2	0	0
1	.	9	2	5

When you see the addends in a place-value chart, you can see that you can add 0s before the first digit in a decimal or after the last digit after a decimal to help you keep the place values straight.

You would get a completely different answer if you ignored the decimals and added 375 + 35 + 12.

The same is true for subtraction.

Ones	.	Tenths $\frac{1}{10}$	Hundredths $\frac{1}{100}$	Thousandths $\frac{1}{1,000}$
2	.	0	0	0
1	.	9	2	5
0	.	0	7	5

Reflect

1 What is the difference between adding whole numbers and adding decimals?

_____

_____

_____

_____

Read the problem below. Then explore how to add more than two addends that have decimals to the thousandths with different numbers of digits.

Maura is going on a plane. She can't have a carry-on backpack that weighs more than 10 pounds. She weighed the items she wants to pack on a sensitive scale: book 5.142 pounds, jacket 3.6 pounds, backpack 1.28 pounds. What is the total weight of these items?

Estimate It

You can round each decimal fraction up or down and then add them together in your head. For example, 5.142 is close to 5, 3.6 is close to 4, and 1.2 is close to 1.

Picture It

Ones	.	Tenths $\frac{1}{10}$	Hundredths $\frac{1}{100}$	Thousandths $\frac{1}{1,000}$
5	.	1	4	2
3	.	6		
1	.	2	8	
	.			

Model It

Use the place-value chart to line up the decimal points.

$$\begin{array}{r} 5.142 \\ 3.600 \\ +\,1.280 \\ \end{array}$$

🔍 Connect It

Now solve the problem.

2 Look at Estimate It on the previous page. What is an estimate of the total weight?

_____ Explain your reasoning. _____

_____

3 How does the place-value chart help you add decimals?

_____

4 How can you add decimals without a place-value chart to make sure you are adding

the same place values? _____

5 Find the sum. Explain how you know that your answer is reasonable.

$$\begin{array}{r} 5.142 \\ 3.600 \\ +\ 1.280 \\ \hline \end{array}$$

_____

6 Does Maura's backpack weigh less than 10 pounds?

_____

7 Explain how to add decimals to the thousandths.

_____

✏️ Try It

Use what you just learned to solve these problems. Show your work on a separate sheet of paper.

8 Aaron's family has several gold items they want to melt down to make a gold bar. There is a spoon that weighs 124.414 grams, a broken necklace that weighs 108.86 grams, and an earring that weighs 15.5 grams. How much is the total weight of the gold? _____

9 Nicky is trying to drink 2.5 liters of water a day. She drank 0.878 liters after breakfast, 1.2 liters after lunch, and 0.75 liters before dinner. How much did she drink all together? _____

Read the problem below. Then explore how to subtract decimals to the thousandths with different numbers of digits.

> Walter wanted to compare the great pitcher Walter Johnson's earned run average to other great pitchers to find out how much lower it was. A lower ERA is better than a higher ERA. He found these pitchers' lifetime ERA statistics.
>
> Walter Johnson 2.167
>
> Sandy Koufax 2.76
>
> How much better was Walter Johnson's ERA than Sandy Koufax's?

Estimate It

You can round each decimal fraction up or down and then compare them in your head. For example, 2.167 is close to 2.2 and 2.76 is close to 2.8.

Picture It

Ones	.	Tenths $\frac{1}{10}$	Hundredths $\frac{1}{100}$	Thousandths $\frac{1}{1,000}$
2	.	7	6	
2	.	1	6	7
	.			

Model It

Use the place-value chart to line up the decimal points.

$$
\begin{array}{r}
2.760 \\
-2.167 \\
\end{array}
$$

Part 3: Guided Instruction

Connect It

Now solve the problem.

10 Look at the Estimate It on the previous page. What is an estimate of the difference?

_____ Explain your reasoning. _____

11 How is subtracting decimals similar to adding decimals?

_____

_____

12 Why is it important to pay attention to 0 in the subtraction problem?

_____

_____

13 How much better was Walter Johnson's ERA than Sandy Koufax's? Find the difference in Model It on the previous page. Explain how you know that your answer is reasonable.

_____

14 What is a way to check your answer?

_____

15 Compare subtracting decimals and subtracting whole numbers.

_____

_____

_____

16 Explain how to subtract decimals to the thousandths.

_____

Try It

Use what you just learned to solve these problems.

17 Sandy Koufax has a 0.655 win/loss percentage; Walter Johnson's is 0.599. How much higher is Koufax's win/loss percentage than Johnson's? _____

18 Tyrone needs to take 4.5 milliliters of cough syrup but only has 2.745 milliliters. How much more does he need for a full dose? _____

Study the student model below. Then solve problems 19–21.

In this problem you have to line up the decimals and express the minuend in a way to make it easier to subtract.

Student Model

Alex's family went on a hike at Mt. Rainier National Park in Washington.

The Silver Falls Trail is a total of 3.1 miles. They hiked 1.534 miles and reached Silver Falls. How much farther do they have to hike to complete the trail?

Look at how you could set up this equation, aligning the decimals.

$$\begin{array}{r} \scriptstyle 2\ \ 10\ 9\ 10 \\ 3.\cancel{1}\cancel{0}\cancel{0} \\ -\ 1.534 \\ \hline 1.566 \end{array}$$

Solution: __1.566 miles__

Pair/Share

What would happen if we did not align the decimal points?

Pair/Share

What do you do when you have addends with different numbers of digits before and after the decimal?

19 A cheetah can run 112.654 kilometers per hour. A pronghorn antelope can run 98.17 kilometers per hour. How much faster is the cheetah than the antelope?

Show your work.

Pair/Share

Does putting the first digit before the decimal and the last digit after the decimal help you align the decimals?

Solution: _____

20 Becky wanted to grow out her hair. She measured the growth each month. The first month her hair grew 1.775 centimeters. The next month it grew 1.45 centimeters. The third month it grew 1.2 centimeters. How many centimeters did her hair grow in the three months?

Show your work.

How can you align decimal points when you have more than one addend?

Solution: _____

Pair/Share

What mistake would I have made if I got 1,932 centimeters?

21 On a field trip, a 6th grade class traveled 19.955 kilometers by train, 7 kilometers by bus, and 2.3 kilometers by car. How far did they travel all together?

A　19,985 kilometers

B　22.955 kilometers

C　29.255 kilometers

D　1.12985 kilometers

Evan chose **A** as the correct answer. How did he get that answer?

How can the position of the decimal point change the value of tens and ones?

_____

_____

_____

_____

Pair/Share

Talk about the problem and then write your answer together.

Solve the problems.

1 Alice has three boxes to carry. One is 1.453 kilograms. One is 3.8 kilograms. One is 11.39 kilograms. What is the total weight?

A 2,630 kilograms

B 16.643 kilograms

C 15.1643 kilograms

D 0.6392 kilograms

2 Seth had a 1.5-liter bottle of tomato juice. He drank some. There was 0.895 liter left when his sister, Beth, came to get a snack. How much did Seth drink?

A −745 liters

B −880 liters

C 0.745 liter

D 0.605 liter

3 Ally needs 30 meters of wood to build a large wooden frame. She bought three different lengths of wood measuring 12.5, 11.43, and 7.244 meters. Choose True or False for each statement.

A Ally has, in total, 30.564 meters of wood to use for the frame. ☐ True ☐ False

B After she builds the frame, Ally will have 1.154 meters of wood left. ☐ True ☐ False

C Ally bought more wood than she needed in order to build the frame. ☐ True ☐ False

D The total wood Ally bought is 1.154 meters less than the amount needed for the frame. ☐ True ☐ False

4   Sammy, Teddy, and Ursula ran a 100-meter race. Sammy's time was 15.03 seconds. Teddy's and Ursula's times were 14.7 seconds and 15.003 seconds, respectively. Which statement is true? Circle all that apply.

A   Teddy ran 0.04 second faster than Ursula.

B   Teddy came in 3rd place.

C   Ursula ran 0.027 second faster than Sammy.

D   The time between the slowest and fastest run was 0.33 second.

5   Kay was trying to triple a salsa recipe. Her recipe for one batch called for 1.232 milliliters of red hot pepper sauce. She thought she added three of that amount for three batches. When people dipped into the salsa, it was too spicy to eat. What could she have done wrong?

_____

_____

6   Stacey answered the problem below incorrectly.

   $16.007 - 0.55 = 10.507$

Describe what she might have done wrong, why her answer doesn't make sense, and then solve the problem correctly.

Show your work.

_____

_____

_____

_____

 **Self Check**   *Go back and see what you can check off on the Self Check on page 51.*

Lesson 10   Part 1: Introduction 👥

Multiply and Divide Decimals

CCSS
6.NS.B.3

You've learned about place value. You've also learned how to multiply and divide decimals to the hundredths. In this lesson, you will multiply and divide decimals to thousandths. Take a look at this problem.

> Ben wants to buy a baseball cap that costs $24.50. The state and sales tax is 8%, or 0.08. How much will he pay in sales tax?

🔍 Explore It

Use the math you already know to solve the problem.

▪ How would you estimate the amount of sales tax?

_____

_____

▪ You can write 24.50 as 24.5. What is 24.5 as a fraction? _____

▪ What is 0.08 as a fraction? _____

▪ How could you show the problem using fractions? _____

▪ Multiply the fractions. What is the tax? _____

▪ Write the tax as a decimal. _____

▪ Does your answer make sense? Explain.

_____

▪ Explain how you could find the amount of sales tax Ben will pay.

_____

_____

Find Out More

You multiply decimals in the same way you multiply whole numbers. You just need to think about where to place the decimal point in the product.

You can think about multiplying fractions to make sense of multiplying decimals.

$$\frac{245}{10} \times \frac{8}{100} = \frac{1,960}{1,000}$$

The denominator is in the thousandths because tenths × hundredths = thousandths. $\left(\frac{1}{10} \times \frac{1}{100} = \frac{1}{1,000}\right)$

$$
\begin{array}{rl}
24.5 & \text{1 decimal place} \\
\times\ 0.08 & +\ \text{2 decimal places} \\
\hline
1.960 & \text{3 decimal places}
\end{array}
$$

The number of decimal places in the product equals the sum of the number of decimal places in the factors.

Reflect

1 Explain why $0.02 \times 0.3 = 0.006$.

_____

_____

_____

Read the problem below. Then explore how to multiply decimals to thousandths.

Four 6th graders are working on a project. They are going to paint a large banner and need to protect the floor. They measured the floor, which is 3.05 meters by 3.658 meters. How many square meters of plastic do they need to cover the entire floor?

Estimate It

You can estimate the product.

3.05 meters is close to 3 meters.

3.658 meters is close to 4 meters.

3×4

Model It

You can think about fractions to place the decimal point.

$3.05 = 3\frac{5}{100}$ or $\frac{305}{100}$

$3.658 = 3\frac{658}{1,000}$ or $\frac{3,658}{1,000}$

$\frac{305}{100} \times \frac{3,658}{1,000}$

Model It

You can use an algorithm to multiply.

Multiply as you would whole numbers.

$$\begin{array}{r} 3.658 \\ \times\ 3.05 \\ \hline 18290 \\ 0000 \\ 10974 \\ \hline \end{array}$$ 3 decimal places
2 decimal places

Connect It

Use what you know about decimals and place value to solve the problem.

2 Look at Estimate It. About how many square meters of plastic will they need?

_____

3 Look at the first Model It. What will the denominator of the product be?

_____

4 Look at the second Model It. How many decimal places will be in the product? How do you know?

_____

_____

5 Add the partial products and place the decimal point in the product in the second Model It. Does your answer make sense?

_____

6 Explain how to multiply decimals.

_____

_____

Try It

Use what you just learned about multiplying with decimals to solve these problems. Show your work on a separate sheet of paper.

7 Madeline studies honeybees. Every week she weighs the same honeybee hive. The first week the hive weighs 11.607 kilograms. Its weight increases about 0.204 kilograms every week. At this rate, how many kilograms will it increase in 7.5 weeks? _____

8 Your fingernails grow at an average rate of 2.25 inches per year. If they grew at an average rate, you never cut them, and they did not break, how long would your fingernails be in 4.5 years? _____

Read the problem below. Then explore how to divide by decimals.

Olympic National Park is 28.5 miles from Forks, Washington. It took the Pearce family 0.75 hours to drive there. What was their average speed, in miles per hour?

Estimate It

You can estimate the quotient.

28.5 miles is close to 30 miles.

0.75 hours is close to 1 hour.

The average speed is about 30 miles ÷ 1 hour.

Model It

Since the fraction bar means division, you can write the division problem as a fraction to understand how to divide by decimals.

$$28.5 \div 0.75 = \frac{28.5}{0.75}$$

To get a whole number divisor, multiply 0.75 by 100. The decimal point moves 2 places to the right. If you multiply the denominator by 100, you also have to multiply the numerator by 100.

$$\frac{28.5}{0.75} \times \frac{100}{100} = \frac{2,850}{75}$$

28.5 ÷ 0.75 is equivalent to 2,850 ÷ 75.

The divisor has two decimal places. Moving the decimal point 2 places to the right to get a whole number is the same as multiplying the divisor by 100. If you multiply the divisor by 100, you have to do the same to the dividend.

$$0.\underset{\smile}{7}5 \overline{\smash{)}28.\underset{\smile}{5}0}$$

$$
\begin{array}{r}
38 \\
75 \overline{\smash{)}2850} \\
-\ 225 \\
\hline
600 \\
-\ 600 \\
\hline
0
\end{array}
$$

Connect It

Use what you know about equivalent fractions and division to solve the problem.

9 Look at Estimate It. About how many miles per hour is their average speed?

_____

10 Look at Model It. Why do you multiply 0.75 by 100?

_____

11 Why do you have to multiply 28.5 by 100?

_____

_____

12 What is the Pearce family's average speed?

_____

13 Does your answer make sense? Explain how you know.

_____

_____

14 Explain how to divide when the divisor is a decimal.

_____

_____

_____

Try It

Use what you just learned about dividing by decimals to solve these problems. Show your work on a separate sheet of paper.

15 At a craft fair, Emily made $52.50 selling paper flowers. If she sold the flowers for $0.75 each, how many paper flowers did she sell? _____

16 Every day Marco puts $0.25 cents into a jar for savings. One day he counted his money and found he had $91.75. How many days had he been saving? _____

Read the problem below. Then explore how to divide decimals using an algorithm.

The average walking speed is 3.4 miles per hour. How many hours would it take to walk from Boston to Seattle, a distance of 3,020.22 miles?

Estimate It

You can estimate the quotient.

3.4 miles per hour is about 3 miles per hour.

3,020.22 miles is about 3,000 miles.

3,000 miles ÷ 3 miles per hour = number of hours

Model It

You can think about equivalent fractions to understand the division algorithm.

$$3,020.22 \div 3.4 = \frac{3,020.22}{3.4}$$

$$\frac{3,020.22}{3.4} \times \frac{10}{10} = \frac{30,202.2}{34}$$

$$3.4\overline{)3020.22}$$

```
          888.3
   34 ) 30202.2
      − 272
        300
      − 272
        282
      − 272
        102
      − 102
          0
```

Connect It

Use what you know about equivalent fractions and dividing by decimals to solve the problem.

17 Look at Estimate It. About how many hours would it take to walk from Boston to Seattle?

_____

18 Look at the fractions in Model It. Why do you multiply the numerator and denominator by 10?

_____

_____

19 Explain how moving the decimal point one place to the right is the same as multiplying the numerator and denominator of the fraction.

_____

_____

20 How many hours would it take to walk from Boston to Seattle? And, how can your estimate help you decide where to place the decimal point?

_____

_____

21 How do you divide by decimals?

_____

_____

Try It

Use what you just learned to solve these problems. Show your work on a separate sheet of paper.

22 Annette had a 24-karat gold necklace that weighs 2.3 grams. She sold it for $123.51. What was the price per gram of her necklace? _____

23 At maturity, a stalk of corn is 76.56 inches tall. It took 2392.5 hours to reach that height. What was the rate of growth per hour? _____

Study the student model below. Then solve problems 24–26.

Student Model

The student multiplied as with whole numbers and used estimation to place the decimal point.

The greatest skateboarding speed recorded is 78.37 mph by Roger Hickey in 1990. If he could keep up that speed for 15 minutes or 0.25 hour, how far could he go?

Look at how you can use estimation to place the decimal point.

15 minutes is $\frac{1}{4}$ of an hour, and 78.37 rounds up to 80, so I can expect my answer to be about $\frac{1}{4}$ of 80, or 20.

$$
\begin{array}{r}
78.37 \\
\times\ 0.25 \\
\hline
39185 \\
15674 \\
\hline
19.5925
\end{array}
$$

Since I know that the answer is going to be around 20, the decimal point belongs after the 19.

Solution: ____19.5925 miles, which is about 20 miles.____

⬤Pair/Share

What is another way to determine where to put the decimal point?

Can you estimate the product?

24 By the age of 21, the best violinists and pianists will have practiced at least 10,000 hours. If you practice an instrument 45 minutes (or 0.75 hours) a day for 365.25 days, the length of a year, how many hours will you have practiced?

Show your work.

⬤Pair/Share

Without doing any multiplication, how can you tell whether the answer will be greater or less than 365.25 hours?

Solution: _____

25 When the Dixon family traded in their old car, it had 53,790 miles on it. They had the car for 8.25 years. On average, how many miles did they drive per year?

Show your work.

How many decimal place values are there in the divisor?

Solution: _____

**Pair/Share**

How could you check your answer?

26 In 1970, a record 1.5 inches of rain fell in one minute at Basse Terre, Guadeloupe in the Caribbean. At this rate, how much rain fell in 3 seconds or 0.05 of a minute? Circle the letter of the correct answer.

A   3 inches

B   0.075 inch

C   0.75 inch

D   30 inches

Evan chose **D** as the correct answer. How did he get that answer?

_____

_____

_____

_____

Will the answer be greater than or less than 1.5 inches?

Pair/Share

Does Evan's answer make sense?

Solve the problems.

1 In 1892 a world record was set. France's M. Garisoain walked on stilts for 4.97 miles from Bayonne to Biarritz, France, at an average speed of 7.10 miles per hour. How long did it take him to walk that distance?

A 70 hours

B 7 hours

C 0.7 hour

D 0.07 hour

2 Maria walks a round-trip of 0.75 mile to school every day. How many miles will she walk in 4.5 days?

A 0.3375 mile

B 3.375 miles

C 33.75 miles

D 337.5 miles

3 Mika babysat for the Tylers for 3.5 hours. They gave her $26.25. How much did she make per hour?

A $0.75 per hour

B $7.50 per hour

C $9.80 per hour

D $13.33 per hour

4 Look at each expression. Is it equivalent to 34.7 × 2.03? Select Yes or No for expressions A–E.

A   3.47 × 20.3   ☐ Yes   ☐ No

B   34.7 + 35.741   ☐ Yes   ☐ No

C   0.347 × 203.0   ☐ Yes   ☐ No

D   3.47 × 2.03   ☐ Yes   ☐ No

E   34.7 + 20.3   ☐ Yes   ☐ No

5 One of Mr. Edward's students answered the following problem on her homework.

17.06 × 25.1 = 42.8206

Part A

Explain to Mr. Edwards whether or not the student got the question correct, and explain the reason why.

_____

_____

_____

Part B

Use the multiplication algorithm to find the answer to the same question.

17.06 × 25.1 = ?

Show your work.

Answer _____

✓ **Self Check** *Go back and see what you can check off on the Self Check on page 51.*

Lesson 11   Part 1: Introduction 👥

Common Factors and Multiples

In earlier grades, you learned about factors. In this lesson you will learn about common factors and multiples. Take a look at this problem.

Matt is running for student council. His friends are going to help him give out 15 posters and 6 banners. Matthew plans to pack all of the posters and banners in boxes. He wants to put the same number of posters and the same number of banners in each box. What is the greatest number of boxes Matthew can pack?

🔍 Explore It

Use the math you already know to solve this problem.

- You know that Matt wants to pack the same number of posters in each box. There are four ways he can pack the 15 posters.

  If he uses 1 box, he will pack it with 15 posters.

  If he uses 3 boxes, he will pack it with _____ posters.

  If he uses 5 boxes, he will pack it with _____ posters.

  If he uses 15 boxes, he will pack it with _____ poster.

- Matt also wants to pack the same number of banners in each box. There are four ways to pack the 6 banners.

  If he uses 1 box, he will pack it with _____ banners.

  If he uses _____ boxes, he will pack it with _____ banners.

  If he uses _____ boxes, he will pack it with _____ banners.

  If he uses _____ boxes, he will pack it with _____ banner.

- Explain how you could find the greatest number of boxes Matthew can pack that have the same number of posters and the same number of banners.

  _____

  _____

  _____

🔍 Find Out More

The number of boxes and the number of equal groups of posters are factors. The product is the total number of posters, 15. In Explore It, you listed all of the factor pairs of 15.

The number of boxes and the number of equal groups of banners are factors. The product is the total number of banners, 6. In Explore It, you listed all of the factor pairs of 6.

When you found the greatest number of boxes that Matthew can pack, you found the **greatest common factor** (GCF) of 15 and 6. The greatest common factor of any two numbers is the greatest factor both numbers have in common. In the problem on the previous page, you found that 3 is the GCF of 15 and 6.

When two numbers have a common factor, like 15 and 6, you can write their sum as a product using the distributive property.

Write each number with 3 as a factor: $15 + 6 = (3 \times 5) + (3 \times 2)$

Use the distributive property. $= 3(5 + 2)$

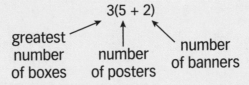

greatest number of boxes   number of posters   number of banners

You can check that $15 + 6 = 3(5 + 2)$

$$21 = 15 + 6$$

$$21 = 21$$

✏️ Reflect

1 Explain how you could use the greatest common factor of 8 and 20 and the distributive property to write $8 + 20$ as a product.

_____

_____

Read the problem below. Then explore how to find the greatest common factor (GCF) of two numbers to solve problems.

Alisha is putting cheese cubes and crackers onto small plates. She has 24 cubes of cheese and 40 crackers. She wants both cheese and crackers on each plate and each plate must have the same number of cheese cubes and the same number of crackers. What is the greatest number of plates she can make using all the cheese and crackers?

 **Model It**

You can list the factors of each number and circle the common factors.

Factors of 24	Factors of 40
(1)	(1)
(2)	(2)
3	(4)
(4)	5
6	(8)
(8)	10
12	20
24	40

Model It

You can make a table to show all of the factors.

Cheese

Number of Plates	1	2	3	4	6	8	12	24
Number of Cheese Cubes	24	12	8	6	4	3	2	1

Crackers

Number of Plates	1	2	4	5	8	10	20	40
Number of Crackers	40	20	10	8	5	4	2	1

Connect It

Now you will solve the problem using the models on the previous page.

2 Look at the list of factors on the previous page. What are the common factors of 24

and 40? _____ What is the greatest common factor? _____

3 Look at the tables on the previous page. Can Alisha make ten plates of cheese and

crackers? Why or why not? _____

_____ Can Alisha make four plates of cheese and crackers? Why or

why not? _____

4 What is the greatest number of plates that Alisha can make if she uses all of the

cheese and crackers? Explain your reasoning. _____

_____

5 What does the greatest common factor represent in this situation? _____

_____

Try It

Use what you just learned about GCF to solve these problems.

6 Amanda is making flower arrangements. She has 20 daisies and 16 roses. Each
arrangement must have the same number of daisies and the same number of roses.
She wants to use all the flowers. What is the greatest number of arrangements she
can make? How many daisies and how many roses will be in each?

_____

7 Use the GCF and distributive property to write 18 + 45 as a product. Then check
your answer.

_____

_____

_____

_____

Read the problem below. Then explore how to find the least common multiple (LCM) of two numbers to solve problems.

> Jackson wants to buy the same number of stamps and envelopes. Stamps are sold in packs of 6. Envelopes are sold in packs of 4. What is the least number of stamps and envelopes Jackson will have to buy?

🔍 Picture It

You can use a number line to help understand the problem.

Multiples of 4 are circled on the top number line.

Multiples of 6 are circled on the bottom number line.

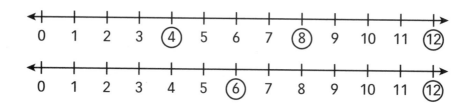

The **least common multiple** (LCM) is the smallest number that is circled on both lines.

🔍 Model It

You can list multiples of each number to help understand the problem. You can circle the common multiples.

Multiples of 4: 4, 8, 12, 16, 20, 24, 28, 32, 36...

Multiples of 6: 6, 12, 18, 24, 30, 36, 42, 48...

The **least common multiple** (LCM) is the smallest number that appears in both lists.

Connect It

Now you will solve the problem using the models on the previous page.

8 Look at Picture It. What multiple is circled on both number lines? _____

What does this mean? _____

9 Look at Model It. What are some common multiples of 4 and 6? _____

10 What do common multiples of 4 and 6 mean in this situation?

_____

_____

11 What is the least common multiple of 4 and 6? Explain your reasoning.

_____

12 What does the least common multiple of 4 and 6 mean in this situation?

_____

_____

13 Explain how to find the least common multiple of two numbers.

_____

_____

Try It

Use what you just learned about LCM to solve these problems. Show your work on a separate sheet of paper.

14 Danny wants to promote his new business. He gave out a free pen to every 4th customer and a free pad of paper to every 7th customer. Which customer will be the first to get both a pen and a pad of paper? _____

15 For exercise, Cindy swims every 6 days and jogs every 8 days. She did both today. How many days from now until she swims and jogs again? _____

Study the student model below. Then solve problems 16–18.

The student found the greatest common factor to solve this problem.

Student Model

Eric is putting together snack bags for his classmates. He bought 18 granola bars and 9 apples. Each snack bag will have the same number of granola bars and apples. Does Eric have enough food to make 10 snack bags?

Look at how you can show your work.

Factors of 18: 1, 2, 3, 6, 9, 18

Factors of 9: 1, 3, 9

Common factors are 1, 3, 9

The GCF is 9.

Solution: _____ No, the greatest number of snack bags Eric can make is 9.

◯Pair/Share

How could you justify your answer with a picture?

How do you find the least common multiple of numbers?

16 Yari wants to make egg biscuits to sell at a fundraiser. Eggs come in packs of 12 and biscuits come in packs of 8. What is the least number of packs of eggs and biscuits Yari can buy to have an equal number of each?

Show your work.

Solution: _____

◯Pair/Share

When do you know you can stop listing multiples to find the LCM?

17 Stacy is planning a vegetable garden. She has 27 tomato plants, 45 bean plants, and 54 carrot plants. Stacy wants each row of her garden to have the same number of each type of plant. What is the greatest number of rows that Stacy can have if she wants to use all of her plants? How many of each type of plant will she have in each row?

Show your work.

Do you need to find the greatest common factor or the least common multiple?

Solution: _____

_____

_____

💬**Pair/Share**

Explain how you can find the GCF of three numbers.

18 Which expression uses the greatest common factor and distributive property to write 18 + 24 as a product? Circle the letter of the correct answer.

A 2(9 + 12)

B 8(10 + 16)

C 6(3) + 6(4)

D 6(3 + 4)

Lily chose **A** as the correct answer. How did she get that answer?

_____

_____

_____

_____

How can you be sure you found the greatest common factor?

💬**Pair/Share**

How can you check that your expression is equivalent to 18 + 24?

Solve the problems.

1 What is the greatest common factor (GCF) of 60 and 90?

A   5

B   15

C   30

D   60

2 What is the least common multiple (LCM) of 10 and 12?

A   120

B   60

C   24

D   2

3 Molly has 24 muffins, 18 breakfast bars, and 12 bottles of juice to be distributed evenly among a certain number of welcome baskets. She wants to package the maximum number of welcome baskets that will contain the same combination of muffins, breakfast bars, and bottles of juice. Which shows the correct number of muffins, breakfast bars, and juice bottles along with the proper explanation? Circle all that apply.

A   12 muffins, 9 breakfast bars, and 6 juice bottles because you divide 24, 18, and 12 by their common factor, which is 2.

B   4 muffins, 3 breakfast bars, and 2 juice bottles because you divide 24, 18, and 12 by 6.

C   3 muffins, 4 breakfast bars, and 6 juice bottles because you divide 24, 18, 12 by their least common multiple, 72.

D   4 muffins, 3 breakfast bars, and 2 juice bottles because you divide 24, 18, 12 by their greatest common factor.

4   The high school's lunch menu repeats every 6 school days. The middle school lunch menu repeats every 8 school days. On March 5th, both schools served chicken wraps. What is the next calendar date on which both schools serve chicken wraps?

March 2013

SU	M	T	W	TH	F	SA
					1	2
3	4	5	6	7	8	9
10	11	12	13	14	15	16
17	18	19	20	21	22	23
24	25	26	27	28	29	30
31						

April 2013

SU	M	T	W	TH	F	SA
	1	2	3	4	5	6
7	8	9	10	11	12	13
14	15	16	17	18	19	20
21	22	23	24	25	26	27
28	29	30				

	MONTH	DATE
Both schools will serve chicken wraps on:		

5   Choose two numbers from this list: 3, 4, 6, 12. Explain the difference between finding the greatest common factor and the least common multiple of the two numbers.

_____

_____

_____

_____

_____

6   Look at the two expressions. Rewrite one expression as a product using the GCF and distributive property. Explain why the other expression cannot be rewritten as a product using the GCF and distributive property.

27 + 45 = _____

23 + 60 = _____

_____

_____

✓ **Self Check**   *Go back and see what you can check off on the Self Check on page 51.*

Lesson 12   Part 1: Introduction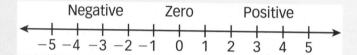

Understand Positive and Negative Numbers

CCSS
6.NS.C.5
6.NS.C.6a
6.NS.C.6c

> **What are positive and negative numbers?**

Positive numbers are greater than 0 and located to the right of 0 on a number line. **Negative numbers** are less than 0 and located to the left of 0 on a number line. The number zero is neither positive nor negative.

```
        Negative        Zero        Positive
    ←——|——|——|——|——|——|——|——|——|——|——|——→
      −5 −4 −3 −2 −1   0   1   2   3   4   5
```

Positive and negative numbers are sometimes called **signed numbers**.

■ Positive numbers can be written with or without a plus sign.

■ Negative numbers are always written with a negative sign.

When solving problems with positive and negative numbers, it important to think about how far from 0 the number is and in what direction.

🔍 **Think**   A thermometer shows positive and negative numbers.

Temperatures above 0 are positive.
Temperatures below 0 are negative.

Look at the thermometer.

20°F is 20 degrees above 0°F.
−20°F is 20 degrees below 0°F.

−30°C is 30 degrees below 0°C.
30°C is 30 degrees above 0°C.

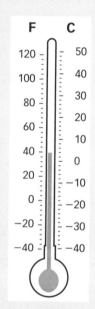

> **Circle the negative numbers labeled on the thermometer.**

🔍 **Think** Every positive and negative number has an opposite.

Numbers that are the same distance from zero but in opposite directions are called **opposite** numbers. Every whole number, fraction, and decimal has an opposite.

The opposite of 4 is −4. Both numbers are the same distance from 0. To plot a point at 4, count 4 units to the right of 0 and draw a point. To plot a point at −4, count 4 units to the left of 0 and draw a point.

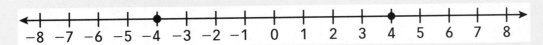

Think about folding the number line in half so that the fold goes through 0. Numbers that line up are opposites.

All the whole numbers and their opposites are called **integers**. All of the numbers labeled on the number line above are integers:

−8, −7, −6, −5, −4, −3, −2, −1, 0, 1, 2, 3, 4, 5, 6, 7, 8

> *The number line shows that zero is its own opposite.*

✏️ **Reflect**

1 Think about the numbers −10 and 10. How could you describe these numbers? What is the same and what is different about these numbers?

_____

_____

_____

_____

🔍 Explore It

A number line can help you understand positive and negative numbers.

Jana and a friend are playing a game that shows a number line from −7 to 7. The game is played with 15 cards numbered with the integers from −7 to 7. Players draw a card from a pile. They earn points for correctly locating the number on the card on the number line and then identifying its opposite.

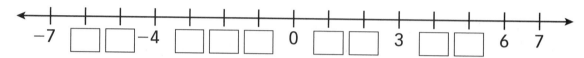

2 Finish labeling the number line.

3 Suppose Jana draws a card that shows −3. Draw a point at −3 on the number line.

4 What number is the opposite of −3? _____. Explain your reasoning.

_____

5 Jana's friend draws a card that shows a 0. Draw a point at 0. What is the opposite of 0?

_____ Explain. _____

6 The next card drawn is −6. How far from 0 is −6? _____ In which direction?

_____ Draw a point at −6.

7 What number is the same distance from 0 as −6 but in the other direction? _____

8 Two numbers that are the same distance from 0 but on different sides of zero are

called _____ numbers.

Now try this problem.

9 Graph each integer and its opposite on the number line below.

     5   −1   4   −2

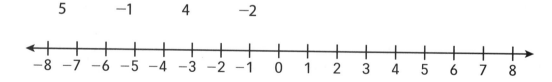

🗨 Talk About It

Solve the problems below as a group.

10 Look at the number lines on the previous page. There are numbers between the numbers you graphed. Just as whole numbers can be positive or negative, fractions and decimals can also be positive and negative.

The number 1.5 is between 1 and 2. The number −1.5 is between −2 and −1. Draw a point at 1.5 and a point at −1.5 on the number line below. Label each point with its value.

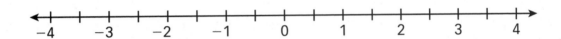

11 How is locating −1.5 on a number line the same as locating 1.5 on a number line?

How is it different? _____

_____

12 Use the number line below to graph the following numbers. Label each point with its value. Then graph and label the opposite of each number.

$$1\frac{1}{2} \qquad -1\frac{1}{4} \qquad -\frac{1}{2}$$

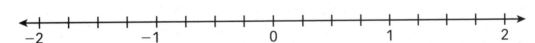

✏ Try It Another Way

Work with your group to explore writing positive and negative numbers to represent a situation.

13 Write a positive or a negative number to represent each situation.

A you owe $25 _____

B a team has a gain of 20 yards in a football game _____

C two floors below ground level _____

D 15 degrees above 0°C _____

E a stock price fell 4.26 points _____

💡 Connect It

Talk through these problems as a class, then write your answers below.

14 Conclude: What number is the opposite of the opposite of 5? What can you say about the opposite of the opposite of a number?

_____

_____

_____

15 Interpret: Positive and negative numbers can show an amount above or below zero. They can also be used to show an amount above or below a certain point.

Students at Taft Middle School have a goal of collecting 1,000 pounds of recycling materials each month. The following table shows their results over a 6-month time period. Complete the table. The first month is done for you.

Month	Pounds Collected	Compared to 1,000	
January	985	**−15**	←15 less than 1,000
February	1,010		
March	995		
April	1,050		
May	975		
June	980		

16 Analyze: Look at the number line below. The letters *a*, *b*, *c*, and *d* all represent integers.

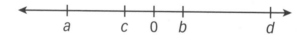

A Which letters represent negative integers? _____ How do you know?

_____

B Which letters represent positive integers? _____ How do you know?

_____

C If *b* and *c* are the same distance from 0, how can you describe them?

_____

Put It Together

17 Use what you have learned to complete this task.

Write a problem about a real-life situation involving temperature or money. The situation should include a number and its opposite that results in an answer of zero.

A Write your problem.

_____

_____

_____

B Graph the numbers you used in your problem on a number line.

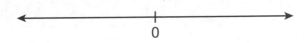

0

_____

C Explain what zero means in this situation.

_____

D What can you say about the sum of a number and its opposite?

_____

Lesson 13   Part 1: Introduction 👥

Absolute Value and Ordering Numbers

CCSS

6.NS.C.5
6.NS.C.7a
6.NS.C.7b
6.NS.C.7c
6.NS.C.7d

In Lesson 12, you learned how to locate positive and negative numbers on a number line. In this lesson you will learn how to compare the numbers and find their absolute value. Take a look at this problem.

The elevation of an object tells you its distance above or below sea level. Negative numbers are used to represent objects below sea level. Positive numbers are used to represent objects above sea level.

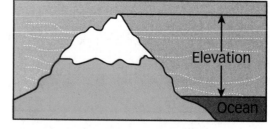

The table below shows the elevations of four objects. Graph their locations on a number line. Describe the distances of the objects above or below sea level.

Object	Mountain	Fish	Sunken Ship	Airplane
Elevation (in km)	2	−1	−4	4

🔍 Explore It

Use the math you already know to solve the problem.

- Sea level is marked and labeled on the number line. Mark and label the elevation of the objects listed in the table above on the number line.

- How far above sea level is the mountain? _____

- How far below sea level is the school of fish? _____

- Is the airplane above or below sea level? _____

- What two objects are the same distance from sea level? Explain how you know.

  _____

- Explain how you could find the distances of the objects from sea level.

  _____

Find Out More

When you answered how far each object is from sea level, you found the absolute value of a number.

The **absolute value** of a number is its distance from 0 on the number line.

|−4| means the absolute value of −4.

−4 is 4 units from 0.

|−4| = 4

The absolute value of −4 is 4 because −4 is 4 units from 0 on the number line.

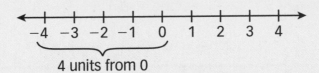

4 units from 0

Absolute value represents distance, so its value is always greater than or equal to 0.

The absolute value of 0 is 0, or |0| = 0.

The farther a number is from 0, the greater the number's absolute value.

In real-world situations, the absolute value of a number is often used to describe the situation. The elevation of the fish is −1 km, but you could also say that the fish is 1 km below sea level. The elevation of the sunken ship is −4 km, but you could also say that the sunken ship is 4 km below sea level.

Reflect

1 Look at your number line on the previous page. Which pair of numbers have the same absolute value? How are the numbers related? Explain.

_____

_____

_____

Read the problem below. Then explore how to use a number line to compare positive and negative numbers.

One morning it was −9°F in Columbus, Ohio and −7°F in Pittsburgh, Pennsylvania. Was it warmer in Columbus or Pittsburgh?

Picture It

You can graph the numbers on a number line.

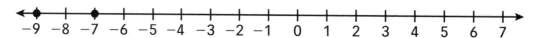

Model It

You can use the number line to write an inequality to compare the numbers.

−9 is to the left of −7 on the number line.
This means that −9 is less than −7.

You can use symbols to compare the numbers.
The symbol < means *is less than*.
−9 < −7

Model It

You can use the number line to write a second inequality to compare the numbers.

−7 is to the right of −9 on the number line.
This means that −7 is greater than −9.

You can use symbols to compare the numbers.
The symbol > means *is greater than*.
−7 > −9

Connect It

Now use the number line and the comparison statements to solve the problem.

2 Look at the number line in Picture It.

Where is −9 located? _____

Where is −7 located? _____

3 From left to right, does the number line show numbers from least to greatest or

greatest to least? _____

4 Which is the warmer temperature, −9°F or −7°F? _____

Which city was warmer? _____

5 Model It shows that you can write two inequalities to compare −9 and −7. Write two inequalities to compare −6 and 5. Tell how you decided.

_____

_____

_____

6 Explain how you can use a number line to compare any two numbers.

_____

_____

Try It

Use what you just learned to compare the numbers below. Use the number line to help if needed.

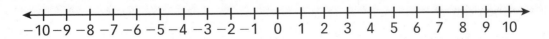

7 Write two inequalities to compare −5 and −3. _____

8 Write two inequalities to compare 9 and −9. _____

Read the problem below. Then explore how to use a number line to order positive and negative numbers.

> Five friends played a game where you earn positive and negative points. Their final scores were −3.5, 2, −3, −1, 1.5. What was the highest score? What was the lowest score?

🔍 Picture It

You can graph the numbers on a number line.

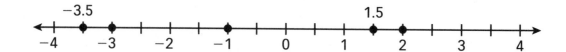

🔍 Model It

You can compare the positions of the numbers on the number line.

−3.5 is to the left of −3.

−3 is to the left of −1.

−1 is to the left of 1.5.

1.5 is to the left of 2.

🔍 Model It

You can compare the positions of the numbers on the number line in another way.

2 is to the right of 1.5.

1.5 is to the right of −1.

−1 is to the right of −3.

−3 is to the right of −3.5.

Connect It

Now use the number line to order the numbers and solve the problem.

9 Look at the first Model It. Order the numbers from least to greatest.

_____

10 Look at the second Model It. Order the numbers from greatest to least.

_____

11 What was the lowest score? How do you know?

_____

12 What was the highest score? How do you know?

_____

13 Explain how to use a number line to order numbers.

_____

_____

_____

Try It

Use what you just learned about ordering numbers to solve these problems. Use a number line to help if needed.

14 Order the numbers from least to greatest.

A $-8, -6, -5, -7$ _____

B $-8.2, 6, -3.5, 8.2, -5$ _____

15 Order the numbers from greatest to least.

A $-\frac{3}{4}, -1, \frac{5}{4}, 2$ _____

B $-0.5, 1.5, 0, -5, 1.25$ _____

Study the student model below. Then solve problems 16–18.

The student graphed the numbers on a number line to order them from least to greatest.

Student Model

A 6th grade class is studying transportation in New York City. They collected this data about the heights above ground and depths below ground of different structures. Write the names of these structures in order from lowest elevation to highest elevation.

Verrazano Narrows Bridge 70 m

Holland Tunnel −25 m

George Washington Bridge 60 m

Lincoln Tunnel −30 m

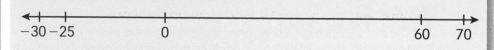

−30 −25   0   60   70

Solution: __Lincoln Tunnel, Holland Tunnel, George Washington__

__Bridge, Verrazano Narrows Bridge__

Pair/Share

Are positive numbers always greater than negative numbers?

Will graphing the numbers on a number line help?

16 Eyeglass prescriptions use positive and negative numbers to describe vision. In general, the farther away from zero the number on a prescription is, the more vision correction you need. Negative numbers mean you are nearsighted, positive numbers mean you are farsighted. The table below shows prescription numbers for five patients.

Patient	A	B	C	D	E
Prescription	−2.25	1.00	−1.50	3.25	−3.00

Which patients are nearsighted?
Which patients are farsighted?

Which patient is the most nearsighted?
Which patient is the most farsighted?

Solution: _____

_____

_____

Pair/Share

How do you compare negative numbers?

17 Which number is greater, −7 or 6? Which number has the greater absolute value, −7 or 6? Explain your thinking. Use comparison symbols and absolute value symbols when you write your answer.

What does absolute value mean?

Solution: _____

_____

_____

_____

_____

Pair/Share

Can a negative number have a greater absolute value than a positive number?

18 The table below shows elevations of different locations in the world. List the elevations in order from greatest to least. Circle the letter of the correct answer.

Are negative numbers always less than positive numbers?

Location	Caspian Sea	Mekong Delta	Lake Eyre	Senegal River	Iron Gate
Elevation (in ft)	−98	230	−52	75	92

A   −52, −98, 75, 92, 230

B   −98, −52, 75, 92, 230

C   230, 92, 75, −52, −98

D   230, 92, 75, −98, −52

Randy chose **B** as the correct answer. How did he get that answer?

_____

_____

_____

_____

Pair/Share

How can you tell that Randy's answer can't be correct by looking at one number's position in his answer?

Solve the problems.

1 The lowest temperatures ever recorded in five of Earth's continents are shown in the table below.

Continent	South America	North America	Antarctica	Europe	Asia
Temperature (in °C)	−39	−66.1	−89.2	−58.1	−68

Which continent has a lower recorded temperature than Asia?

A South America

B North America

C Europe

D Antarctica

2 On February 17, 1936, the following temperatures were recorded:

City	Temperature
McIntosh, SD	−58°F
Duluth, MN	−26°F
Miami, FL	78°F

Choose True or False for each statement.

A The temperature difference between McIntosh, SD, and Duluth, MN, was 84°F.   ☐ True   ☐ False

B Duluth, MN, was 32°F warmer than McIntosh, SD.   ☐ True   ☐ False

C The temperature difference between Miami, FL, and Duluth, MN, was 52°F.   ☐ True   ☐ False

D The temperature difference between the highest and lowest temperatures was 136°F.   ☐ True   ☐ False

3 From the list on the left, write in the correct temperature along the thermometer.

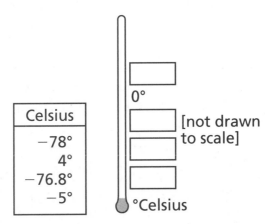

4 A tour group is going sea diving. Sea level is 0 feet. The ocean floor is −18 feet. One diver is already at −11 feet. The tour guide is keeping watch on the deck at 5 feet above sea level directly above the diver. What is the distance from the tour guide to the diver? Draw and label a number line to justify your answer.

Answer _____ feet

5 Look at the number line below. The letters *a, b, c,* and *d* all represent integers.

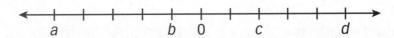

A Write two inequalities to compare *a* and *b*. _____ How do you know?

_____

B Write two inequalities to compare *b* and 0. _____ How do you know?

_____

C If |*a*| = |*d*|, what can you say about *a* and *d*?

_____

✓ **Self Check** *Go back and see what you can check off on the Self Check on page 51.*

Lesson 14   Part 1: Introduction 👥
The Coordinate Plane

You learned how to graph points on a coordinate plane when the coordinates were positive. You know how to locate negative numbers on a number line. Now we'll put these skills together. Take a look at this problem.

Describe the location of points *A*, *B*, *C*, and *D* on the graph to the right.

The point where the number lines intersect is the **origin**. The ordered pair for the origin is (0, 0).

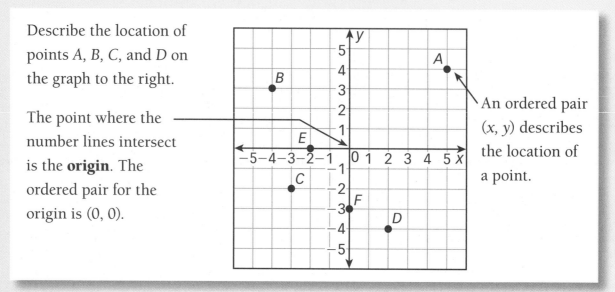

An ordered pair (*x*, *y*) describes the location of a point.

🔍 Explore It

Use the math you already know to solve this problem.

● Place your finger on the origin. Move 5 units to the right and 4 units up. The ordered pair for point *A* is (_____, 4).

● Place your finger on the origin. Move left and up to point *B*. Describe how far left and up point *B* is from (0, 0). _____

The ordered pair for point *B* is (−4, _____).

● Start at (0, 0). Describe how to get to point *C*. What is the ordered pair for point *C*?

_____

The ordered pair for point *C* is _____

● What is the ordered pair for point *D*? _____

● Explain how to locate points on the coordinate plane. _____

_____

Find Out More

On the previous page, you wrote ordered pairs to describe points on a coordinate plane. The *x*-axis and *y*-axis intersect at the origin and divide the coordinate plane into four **quadrants**.

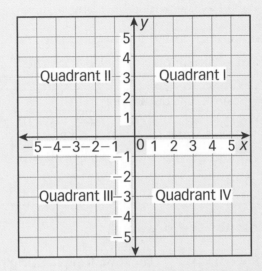

Points *A*, *B*, *C*, and *D* from the previous page are in different quadrants.

Point	Coordinates (x, y)	Quadrant
A	(5, 4)	I
B	(−4, 3)	II
C	(−3, −2)	III
D	(2, −4)	IV

Points *E* and *F* are not in a quadrant.

Point *E* at (−2, 0) is on the *x*-axis. Every point on the *x*-axis has a *y*-coordinate that is 0.

Point *F* at (0, −3) is on the *y*-axis. Every point on the *y*-axis has an *x*-coordinate that is 0.

Reflect

1　Describe the location of a point that has a negative *x*-coordinate and a negative *y*-coordinate.

_____

_____

_____

Read the problem below. Then explore how to graph points on the coordinate plane.

Allyn is a college student. She started her day in her room. Then she attended classes in the Science, Education, and Art buildings. She ate lunch at the dining hall before meeting a friend at the Music building.

The coordinate plane represents a map of Allyn's college campus. Graph each building as a point on a coordinate plane labeled with the first letter of the building.

Building	Science	Education	Art	Dining	Music
Coordinate	(−5, 3)	(−6, 0)	(−2, −5)	(0, −1)	(6, 5)

 **Model It**

You can use words to describe the locations.

Building	Location from the Origin
Science	5 units left, 3 units up
Education	6 units left
Art	2 units left, 5 units down
Dining	1 unit down
Music	6 units right, 5 units up

 **Graph It**

You can graph the ordered pairs to solve the problem.

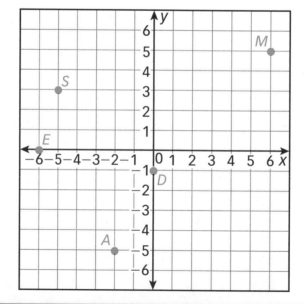

Connect It

Now you will explain how to solve the problem from the previous page using your understanding of how to graph and locate points on a coordinate plane.

2 Why is the origin important when graphing points on the coordinate plane?

_____

3 Look at the ordered pairs and Model It. What does the first coordinate tell you? What does the second coordinate tell you?

_____

_____

4 Allyn's room is located at (3, −3). Use words to describe the location on a coordinate plane.

_____

5 What does it mean when the x-coordinate or y-coordinate of a point is 0?

_____

_____

6 Explain how to graph a point on the coordinate plane.

_____

_____

Try It

Use what you just learned about graphing points on the coordinate plane to solve this problem. Show your work on a separate sheet of paper.

7 Graph and label these locations on a coordinate plane. Explain how each point is related to the origin.

Location	Coordinate
Home	(0, −3)
School	(−2, −3)
Library	(−1, 3)
Park	(2, −3)

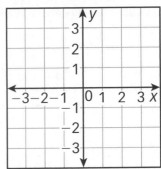

Read the problem below. Then explore how to reflect points in the *x*- and *y*-axis.

Sophia draws three triangles. What is the relationship between the coordinates of triangle *ABC* and triangle *DEF*? What is the relationship between the coordinates of triangle *ABC* and triangle *GHI*?

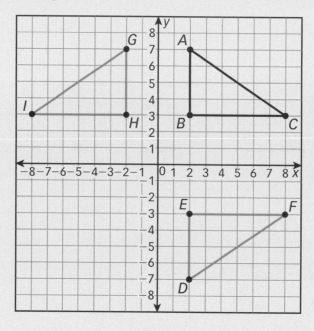

🔍 Picture It

You can list the coordinates of the points of each triangle to understand the problem.

ΔABC	ΔDEF	ΔGHI
A (2, 7)	D (2, −7)	G (−2, 7)
B (2, 3)	E (2, −3)	H (−2, 3)
C (8, 3)	F (8, −3)	I (−8, 3)

Connect It

Now you will solve the problem by analyzing the coordinates.

8 Across which axis do you reflect $\triangle ABC$ to get $\triangle DEF$? _____

9 Look at the coordinates of points A and D on the graph. What is the same? What is different?

_____

10 Compare the coordinates of points B and E and points C and F. How do the coordinates of a point change when it is reflected across the x-axis?

_____

11 Across which axis do you reflect $\triangle ABC$ to get $\triangle GHI$? _____

12 Compare the coordinates of points G and A, points B and H, and points C and I. How do the coordinates of a point change when it is reflected across the y-axis?

_____

_____

Try It

Use what you just learned about reflecting points across the x- and y-axis to solve these problems. Write your answers on the lines below.

13 Brandon draws a reflection of the point $(-4, -6)$. He gets the point $(-4, 6)$. Across which axis did he reflect the point? Explain how you know.

_____

_____

14 Flora reflects the point $(5, -10)$ across the y-axis. What are the coordinates of the reflected point? Explain how you know.

_____

_____

Read the problem below. Then explore how to find the distance between points with the same *x-* or *y*-coordinate.

The coordinate plane below represents where Jenna's friends live. Jenna's apartment is at point *J*. Zac's house is at point *Z*. Each unit on this coordinate plane represents one block. How many blocks does Jenna need to walk to get to Zac's house?

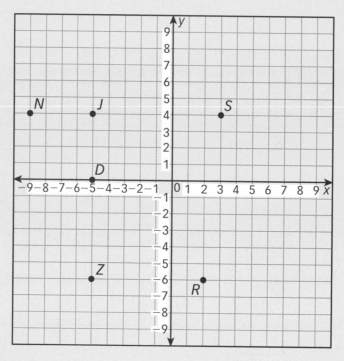

Model It

You can count the units between points to help you understand this problem.

The *x*-coordinates are the same, so you can count the units between the *y*-coordinates. Count from 4 to −6.

Model It

You can use absolute value to help you understand this problem.

You can find the distances of both points from the *x*-axis and add them.

The distance from (−5, 4) to the *x*-axis is |4|.

The distance from (−5, −6) to the *x*-axis is |−6|.

$|4| + |-6| = 4 + 6$

🔍 Connect It

Now you will solve the problem using the models.

15 Look at the first Model It. Count the units from (−5, 4) to (−5, −6). How many blocks are between Jenna's apartment and Zac's house? Explain how you know.

_____

_____

16 Jenna's friend Sam lives at point S. Explain how to count units to find the distance between Jenna's and Sam's apartments.

_____

_____

17 Look at the second Model It. What distance does the |4| and |−6| represent?

_____

18 Explain how to find the distance between points J and Z using absolute value.

_____

_____

19 Explain how to use absolute value to find the distance between two points with the same x-coordinate.

_____

_____

✏️ Try It

Use what you just learned about finding the distance between points to solve this problem. Write your answer on the lines below.

20 Explain how to find the distance between points J and S using absolute value.

_____

_____

Study the student model below. Then solve problems 21–23.

The student located each point on the coordinate plane and found the distance to the y-axis.

On a coordinate plane, Vera's home is at (3, −5) and the park is at (−3, −5). Graph each point on a coordinate plane and find the distance between Vera's home and the skate park. Each unit is 1 mile.

Look at how you can show your work using a model.

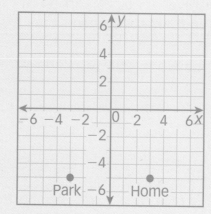

$$|3| + |-3| = 3 + 3$$

Solution: _____6 miles_____

Pair/Share

What else do you notice about these points?

Are the points reflected across the x- or y-axis?

21 Draw △PQR by plotting the points P (−5, 1), Q (−5, 4), R (−1, 4). What is the relationship between △PQR and △JKL?

Show your work.

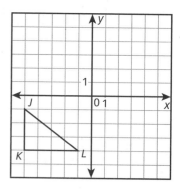

Pair/Share

How can you tell from the ordered pairs if a point is reflected across the x- or y-axis?

Solution: _____

_____

Use this coordinate plane for problems 22 and 23.

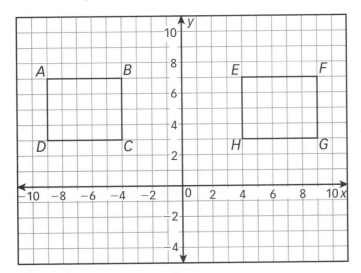

22 Use points *C* and *H* to calculate the distance between the two pools shown on the coordinate plane. Each unit is one meter.

Solution: _____

_____

How many units from the y-axis are the two rectangles?

🗨 **Pair/Share**

What other points could you use to check that the distance is correct?

23 Using the points on the coordinate plane above, which of the following statements is true?

A The distance from *A* to *E* is $|7| + |7|$.

B The distance from *A* to *E* is $|4| + |7|$.

C The distance from *A* to *E* is $|-9| + |7|$.

D The distance from *A* to *E* is $|-9| + |4|$.

Angie chose **A** as the correct answer. Why is her answer incorrect?

_____

_____

_____

Compare the x- and y-coordinates of A and E. Which coordinate is the same? Which is different?

🗨 **Pair/Share**

What other points are the same distance apart as points *A* and *E*?

Solve the problems.

1 Which statement is true about the distance from the food court to the store?

   A   It is equal to 4 units.

   B   It equals the distance from the movie theatre to the arcade.

   C   It is less than the distance from the movie theatre to the arcade.

   D   It is greater than the distance from the movie theatre to the arcade.

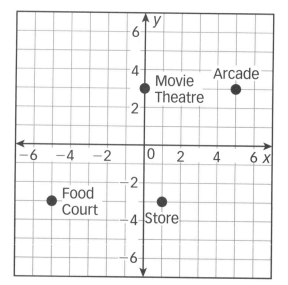

2 A new coffee shop is being built. Its location is the reflection of the arcade's coordinates across the *y*-axis. Which procedure will find the correct distance between the arcade and the new coffee shop? Circle all that apply.

   A   Find the sum of |3| and |3|.

   B   Simplify the expression |−5| + |5|.

   C   Find the distance between (5, 3) and (5, −3).

   D   Find the distance of each point from the *y*-axis and then add.

3 Each lettered point represents a location on the number line. Choose True or False for each statement.

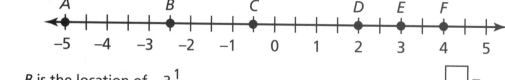

   A   *B* is the location of $-3\frac{1}{2}$.   ☐ True   ☐ False

   B   *C* is a positive number.   ☐ True   ☐ False

   C   *B* and *D* are opposites.   ☐ True   ☐ False

   D   The distance between *A* and *B* is negative.   ☐ True   ☐ False

   E   The absolute value of *A* is greater than the value of *F*.   ☐ True   ☐ False

4   Three points representing the corners of a rectangular garden are *A* (−7, 3), *B* (7, 3), and *C* (7, −3).

Part A

Graph the points representing the corners of the garden. Explain how to find the coordinates of the fourth corner, point *D*. Then graph and label that point.

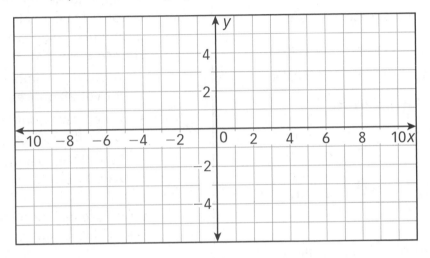

_____

_____

Part B

Name two points that are reflections of each other across the *x*-axis.

_____

Name two points that are reflections of each other across the *y*-axis.

_____

Part C

Find the distance between two points that have the same *y*-coordinate.

_____

 **Self Check**   *Go back and see what you can check off on the Self Check on page 51.*

Solve the problems.

1 Randi has a party-sized sandwich that is $\frac{3}{4}$ yard long. She will cut it into smaller sandwiches that are each $\frac{1}{12}$ yard long. Which expression can be used to determine the number of smaller sandwiches Randi can cut?

A $\frac{12}{1} \div \frac{3}{4}$ **C** $\frac{3}{4} \times \frac{12}{1}$

B $\frac{4}{3} \div \frac{1}{12}$ **D** $\frac{3}{4} \times \frac{1}{12}$

2 A scientist recorded the top flight speed of two peregrine falcons. One flew 306.87 km/h, and the other flew 298.59 km/h. What was the difference between their two speeds?

A   8.28 km/h

B   8.36 km/h

C   16.28 km/h

D   108.36 km/h

3 Which point is the image of point $R(4, -7)$ first reflected across the x-axis and then across the y-axis?

A $(-4, -7)$

B $(-7, -4)$

C $(4, -7)$

D $(-4, 7)$

4 Pricilla's Perfect Pie factory uses a scale to reject pies that are more than 3.2 ounces from the target weight of 28 ounces. The factory's scale is calibrated to show how close a pie weighs to the target weight. The scale will display:

- A positive number if the pie's weight is over 28 ounces.

- A negative number if the pie's weight is less than 28 ounces.

- Zero if the weight is exactly 28 ounces.

Which pie will be rejected by the scale? Select all that apply.

A   A pie with a reading of -2.8 ounces.

B   A pie with a reading of 3.5 ounces.

C   A pie with a reading of -3.3 ounces.

D   A pie with a reading of 28 ounces.

5 From the list below, write a number in each box to create three true mathematical statements. Each number can be used only once.

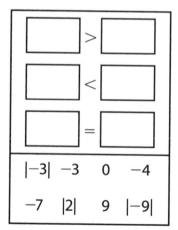

$|-3|$ -3 0 -4

-7 $|2|$ 9 $|-9|$

6 You can use all four quadrants of the coordinate plane when making polygons.

Part A

Draw a rectangle on the grid by plotting the points $(-3, -2)$, $(-3, 3)$, $(6, -2)$, and $(6, 3)$.

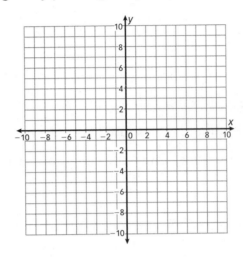

Part B

What are the length and width of the rectangle that you made in Part A?

Answer _____

7 Mr. Novak asked his students to use the distributive property and the greatest common factor (GCF) at the same time to express $18 + 45$ in a different way. Jude and Rachel came up with the expressions below.

Jude: $9(2 + 5)$

Rachel: $3(6 + 15)$

Which student followed Mr. Novak's directions correctly? Explain your answer.

_____

_____

_____

Performance Task

Answer the questions and show all your work on separate paper.

Reema wants to build a coat rack for the front hallway. The wall is 4 feet long, and the piece of wood she has for the rack is $28\frac{1}{4}$ inches long. She wants to center the coat rack on the wall. There needs to be an equal amount of space, about 7 or 8 inches, between the coat hooks. The first and last hooks should be no less than $1\frac{3}{4}$ inches from either end of the wood. How many hooks should Reema use? What is the distance between the hooks? What is the distance of each hook from the left edge of the wood?

Draw and label a diagram of the coat rack on the wall. Mark all the measurements for placing the wood on the wall, and for attaching the hooks on the wood. You can use either fractions or decimals to label and calculate the measurements.

Reflect on Mathematical Practices

After you complete the task, choose one of the following questions to answer.

1. **Model** What models helped you to solve this problem? How did they help?

2. **Be Precise** When was it easier to use fractions, and when was it easier to work with decimal numbers?

Unit 3
Expressions and Equations

Solving a mystery can be fun. Who stole the cookie from the cookie jar? What's behind door number 3? There are many mysteries that you can solve in mathematics, too. Solving a mathematical mystery is sometimes as easy as adding or multiplying some numbers. Other times, the mystery starts by figuring out what the actual math problem is you need to solve. Being able to translate written words to mathematics phrases is an important skill you will learn in this unit.

✓ Self Check

Before starting this unit, check off the skills you know below. As you complete each lesson, see how many more you can check off!

I can:	Before this unit	After this unit
evaluate numerical expressions that contain exponents, for example: $2^4 + 6 = 22$	☐	☐
interpret and evaluate algebraic expressions, for example: $2(8 + 7)$ means twice the sum of 8 and 7	☐	☐
solve equations, for example: if $3 = \frac{1}{2}k$, then $k = 6$	☐	☐
solve inequalities, for example: for example, if $3x \geq 15$, then $x \geq 5$	☐	☐
use equations and inequalities to solve word problems	☐	☐
write equations to show the relationship between a dependent and independent variables	☐	☐

Lesson 15   Part 1: Introduction 👥

Numerical Expressions with Exponents

CCSS
6.EE.A.1

In previous lessons, you learned about powers of 10. Take a look at this problem.

A sports store orders a box of table tennis balls. The dimensions of the box are 10 inches by 10 inches by 10 inches. Inside the box, there are 6 layers of table tennis balls. Each layer is made up of 6 rows and 6 columns of table tennis balls.

How many table tennis balls are in the box?

🔍 Explore It

Use the math you know to solve the problem.

- Write a multiplication expression to represent the volume of the box. _____

- Write the expression you wrote for the volume of the box using exponents. _____

- Write a multiplication expression to represent the number of table tennis balls in one layer of the box. _____

- Write a multiplication expression to represent the number of table tennis balls in all 6 layers of the box. _____

- Write an expression using exponents to represent the total number of table tennis balls in the box. _____

- Explain how you could find the number of table tennis balls in the box.

  _____

🔍 Find Out More

You already know that multiplication is a shorter way to write repeated addition. You use exponents to write repeated multiplication in a shorter way.

	Repeated Addition	Repeated Multiplication
Problem	$5 + 5 + 5 + 5$	$5 \cdot 5 \cdot 5 \cdot 5$
Shorter way to write it	$5 \cdot 4$	5^4
How to read it	5 times 4	5 raised to the fourth power

Numbers raised to the second or third power are often read in specific ways.

5^2 is read "five squared." 5^3 is read "five cubed."

Expressions written with exponents are called **exponential expressions**.
The number being multiplied by itself is called the **base**.
The **exponent** shows how many times you multiply the base by itself.

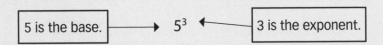

The base of an exponential expression can be any kind of number.

$$7^2 = 7 \cdot 7 \qquad \left(\frac{1}{3}\right)^5 = \frac{1}{3} \cdot \frac{1}{3} \cdot \frac{1}{3} \cdot \frac{1}{3} \cdot \frac{1}{3} \qquad (0.2)^3 = 0.2 \cdot 0.2 \cdot 0.2$$

When you multiply measurements with units, the units are also multiplied. In the example on the previous page, to find the volume of the box, you multiply 10 inches · 10 inches · 10 inches.

$$10 \text{ inches} \cdot 10 \text{ inches} \cdot 10 \text{ inches} = 10^3 \text{ inches}^3$$
$$= 10 \cdot 10 \cdot 10 \text{ inches}^3$$
$$= 1,000 \text{ in.}^3$$

This is why area is measured in square units and why volume is measured in cubic units.

✏️ Reflect

1 Is 2^7 equal to $2 \cdot 7$? Explain.

_____

_____

Read the problem below. Then explore different ways to understand how to write and evaluate expressions with exponents.

Julie's brother says that instead of paying her the $40 he owes her, he will give her $2 today and double the amount she has each day for 6 days. Should Julie accept her brother's offer? Why or why not?

Model It

Use multiplication to represent the problem.

Find the amount of money Julie has each day and then double it to find the amount she has the next day.

Day 1	Day 2	Day 3	Day 4	Day 5	Day 6
2	$2 \cdot 2 = 4$	$4 \cdot 2 = 8$	$8 \cdot 2 = 16$	$16 \cdot 2 = 32$	$32 \cdot 2 = 64$

Model It

Represent the problem with repeated multiplication.

Each day, Julie gets two times the amount of money she got the previous day.

Day	Amount of Money Julie Has from Her Brother
1	2
2	$2 \cdot 2$
3	$2 \cdot 2 \cdot 2$
4	$2 \cdot 2 \cdot 2 \cdot 2$
5	$2 \cdot 2 \cdot 2 \cdot 2 \cdot 2$
6	$2 \cdot 2 \cdot 2 \cdot 2 \cdot 2 \cdot 2$

Connect It

Now you will solve the problem from the previous page by writing a power.

2 Look at the first Model It on the previous page. Why do you double 8 to find the amount of money Julie will have on Day 4? _____

_____

_____

3 Look at the second Model It. How can you tell that the amount from the previous day is being doubled? _____

_____

_____

4 In the second Model It, which expression represents the amount of money Julie will have on Day 6? _____

5 How can you write an expression for the amount of money Julie has on Day 6 using exponents? _____

6 How much money will Julie have on Day 6? Should she take her brother's offer? Explain.

_____

_____

7 Matt thinks that if Julie starts with $2, she will have $12 after 6 days. Explain what Matt is doing wrong.

_____

_____

Try It

Use what you just learned to solve these problems. Show your work on a separate sheet of paper.

8 Maria is buying new carpet for her bedroom. Her bedroom is in the shape of a square and the length of each side is 12 feet. Write and simplify an exponential expression to find how much carpet she needs. _____

_____

9 Write and simplify a multiplication expression to represent 5^4. _____

Read the problem below. Then explore different ways to understand evaluating expressions with exponents.

Michael, Morgan, and Keegan are in the same class. The teacher asks the students to write and simplify the expression "6 plus 4 cubed." Here are the expressions each person wrote.

Michael	Morgan	Keegan
$(6 + 4)^3$	$6^3 + 4^3$	$6 + 4^3$

Which students will get the correct answer? Which, if any, of the expressions are equivalent? Explain.

🔍 Model It

Use the order of operations to simplify Michael's expression.

First add 6 and 4. $6 + 4 = 10$

Then raise 10 to the third power. $10^3 = 10 \cdot 10 \cdot 10$

🔍 Model It

Use the order of operations to simplify Morgan's expression.

First find 6^3 and 4^3. $6^3 = 6 \cdot 6 \cdot 6$ $4^3 = 4 \cdot 4 \cdot 4$

                          $= 216$ $= 64$

Then add 6^3 and 4^3. $216 + 64$

🔍 Model It

Use the order of operations to simplify Keegan's expression.

First find 4^3. $4^3 = 4 \cdot 4 \cdot 4$

                          $= 64$

Then add 6. $64 + 6$

✎ **Connect It**

Now you will solve the problem from the previous page using the order of operations with exponents.

10 Look at Michael's expression. Why do you add 6 + 4 first?

_____

11 Look at Morgan's expression. Why do you simplify each exponential expression first?

_____

12 The teacher says the expression equals 70. Which student wrote the expression correctly? _____

13 How might the teacher have said the expression if she wanted students to write Michael's expression? _____

14 Corwin tries to evaluate $4^2 \cdot 5 + 6$, as shown below.

$4^2 \cdot 5 + 6$

$= 4^2 \cdot 11$ ✗

$= 16 \cdot 11$

$= 176$

Explain why his answer is incorrect. _____

_____

✎ **Try It**

Use what you just learned to solve these problems.

15 Evaluate: $\frac{6^2}{3}$ _____

16 Evaluate: $3 + 5^2 \cdot 4$ _____

Study the student model below. Then solve problems 17–19.

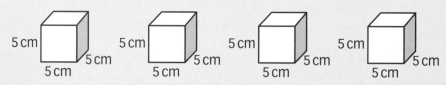

The volume of 4 cubes is 4 times the volume of 1 cube.

Write and evaluate an expression using exponents to find the total volume of the 4 cubes shown below.

5 cm   5 cm   5 cm

5 cm   5 cm   5 cm

5 cm   5 cm   5 cm

5 cm   5 cm   5 cm

Look at how you could show your work using labeled equations.

Volume of 1 cube: $= lwh$

$= 5 \text{ cm} \cdot 5 \text{ cm} \cdot 5 \text{ cm}$

$= 5^3 \text{ cm}^3$

Volume of 4 cubes: $V = 4 \cdot 5 \cdot 5 \cdot 5 \text{ cm}^3$

$V = 4 \cdot 125 \text{ cm}^3$

$V = 500 \text{ cm}^3$

Solution: $\underline{V = 4 \cdot 5^3 ; 500 \text{ cm}^3}$

Pair/Share

Is $(4 \cdot 5)^3$ equal to $4 \cdot 5^3$? Why or why not?

What is the relationship between the number of the space and the power that shows the number of grains on that space?

17 In an old story, a man puts 2 grains of rice on the first space of a chess board. He puts 4 grains on the second space, 8 grains on the third space, and so on. Write and evaluate an expression with exponents to find how many grains of rice the man puts on the tenth space.

Show your work.

Pair/Share

What do you think is meant by the phrase "exponential growth"?

Solution: _____

18 Moira does one-half of a homework assignment on Monday. On Tuesday, Wednesday, and Thursday, she does one-half of the homework she has left over from the day before. Write and evaluate an expression using exponents to find the fraction of the original assignment Moira will have to do on Friday in order to completely finish her homework.

Show your work.

Try using a picture to model the assignment.

Solution: _____

19 Evaluate: $\dfrac{(6 + 2)^3 - 12}{5}$

A $\dfrac{2}{5}$

B $90\dfrac{2}{5}$

C 100

D $509\dfrac{3}{5}$

Jerry chose **A** as the correct answer. How did he get that answer?

_____

_____

_____

_____

How does the order of operations apply to evaluating this expression?

Solve the problems.

1 Which *best* describes the first step in evaluating the expression $4 \cdot \dfrac{53 + 1}{(8 - 5)^3}$?

A simplify 5^3

B multiply $4 \cdot 53$

C subtract $8 - 5$

D add $53 + 1$

2 In a science-fiction story, a spaceship travels 3 times faster each minute than it traveled during the minute before. If the ship travels at 3 km/hr during its first minute of flight, which expression shows the ship's speed during the 15th minute?

A $3 \cdot 15$

B 15^3

C 3^{15}

D $3 \cdot 3$

3 From the choices on the left, write inside the box each expression equivalent to $3^4 \times 3^2$.

		Expressions equivalent to $3^4 \times 3^2$.
$3^2 \times 3^4$	3^6	
12×6	$3^3 \times 3^3$	
3^8	81×9	

4 Look at the cube below.

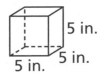

5 in.
5 in.
5 in.

Which statement correctly calculates the volume of the cube? Choose True or False for each statement.

A Simplify the expression $5 + 5 + 5$. ☐ True ☐ False

B Simplify the expression $5 \times 5 \times 5$. ☐ True ☐ False

C Simplify the expression 3×5. ☐ True ☐ False

D Simplify the expression 5×25. ☐ True ☐ False

E Simplify the expression 5^3. ☐ True ☐ False

5 Write each of the numbers 1, 4, 9, 16, and 25 as a base raised to the second power. Explain why these numbers sometimes are called "perfect squares."

_____

_____

_____

6 Trey knows that $3 + 4 = 4 + 3$ and $3 \cdot 4 = 4 \cdot 3$. He says that $3^4 = 4^3$. Is Trey correct? Explain your answer.

_____

_____

_____

✓ Self Check *Go back and see what you can check off on the Self Check on page 143.*

Lesson 16   Part 1: Introduction 👥

Algebraic Expressions

In Lesson 15, you learned to write and evaluate expressions with numbers and operations. Now, take a look at this problem.

Describe the expression $2x + 5$ in words.

🔍 Explore It

Use the math you know to solve the problem.

■ What does the letter x stand for?

_____

■ Which operation is represented by $2x$?

_____

■ What do you call the result of this operation?

_____

■ What operation does the $+$ sign show?

_____

■ What do you call the result of this operation?

_____

■ Explain what the whole expression represents.

_____

_____

_____

Find Out More

You have evaluated expressions with known numbers and operation signs. An example of this would be $6 - 7 \times 4$. Now you will evaluate expressions that include variables. Remember, a **variable** is a letter that stands for an unknown number.

Look at this expression.

variable

coefficient   constant

$$2x + 5$$

term   term

Every expression is made up of terms. A **term** is a known number, a variable, or the product of a known number and variable(s). The expression $2x + 5$ has two terms: $2x$ and 5.

A term that is a known number without variables is called a **constant**. The expression $2x + 5$ has one constant: 5.

A term that includes variables is called a **variable term**. The expression $2x + 5$ has one variable term: $2x$.

If one factor of a variable term is a known number, that number is called the **coefficient**. The coefficient of the term $2x$ is 2.

Look again at the term $2x$. It means "multiply a number by 2." You have used the symbol $\times$ for multiplication. However, now that you are using the variable x, you will need other ways to show multiplication. The expression $2 \times x$ would look confusing. Instead, you can write $2 \cdot x$ or $2x$.

Reflect

1 Claire says the expression $8x^3$ has three terms: 8, x, and 3. Is she correct? Explain.

_____

_____

_____

Read the problem below. Then explore ways to write expressions from words.

> Write an expression with the same meaning as "subtract a number times 4 from 10."

Model It

You can look for operation words to help you write the expression.

"Subtract a number times 4 from 10."
The expression will be a difference between terms.

This is the overall "shape" of the expression.

Model It

You can think of similar expressions to help you write this expression.

Write an expression for "subtract 6 from 10." $10 - 6$

Write an expression for "subtract a number from 10." $10 - x$

Write an expression for "a number times 4." $4x$

🔍 Connect It

Now, you will solve the problem from the previous page using the models.

2 Look at the first Model It on the previous page. When you subtract a number "from 10," will 10 be the first term or the second term? Explain.

_____

3 Erica says that the expression $4x$ has one term. Is she correct? Explain.

_____

4 Look at the second Model It. Write an expression for "subtract a number times 4 from 10." _____

5 List each term in your answer to problem 4. _____

6 Does your answer to problem 4 have any constants? Explain. _____

_____

7 What are the coefficients, if any, in your answer to problem 4? Explain.

_____

8 Explain the difference between a constant and a coefficient.

_____

✏️ Try It

Use what you just learned about writing expressions to solve these problems.

9 Write an expression with the same meaning as "the result of multiplying $\frac{1}{2}$ by a number, then subtracting 9."

_____

10 Write an expression with the same meaning as "7 less than the square of a number."

_____

11 Write an expression to represent "the sum of 3 and the quotient of a number divided by 6."

_____

Read the problem below. Then explore ways to write and evaluate expressions with variables.

Jennifer buys 1 pack of orange sugarless gum and 3 packs of mint sugarless gum. The pack of orange gum has 8 pieces. The packs of mint gum each have the same number of pieces.

● Write an expression to show the total number of pieces of gum that Jennifer buys.

● If 1 pack of mint gum has 6 pieces, what is the total number of pieces of gum that Jennifer buys?

Picture It

You can draw a picture to help you understand this problem.

You can draw the packs of gum and label the number of pieces in each pack.

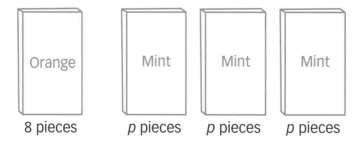

Model It

You can use words to help you solve this problem.

You can write a sentence describing the total number of gum pieces.

The total number of pieces of gum is the sum of the number of pieces in one pack of orange gum and the number of pieces in three packs of mint gum.

The word *sum* in the sentence above tells you that the expression will have this overall "shape."

Connect It

Now you will solve the problem from the previous page using the picture and model.

12 Write an expression for "the number of pieces in one pack of orange gum."

_____

13 Write an expression for "the number of pieces in three packs of mint gum."

_____

14 Write an expression for "the sum of the number of pieces in one pack of orange gum and the number of pieces in three packs of mint gum."

_____

15 Explain how you could use the expression from problem 14 to find the total number of pieces Jennifer buys if each pack of mint gum has 6 pieces.

_____

_____

Try It

Use what you just learned about solving expressions with variables to solve these problems.

16 Martina is 3 inches less than twice as tall as her little brother. Write an expression for Martina's height. How tall is Martina if her little brother is 28 inches tall?

_____

17 Tracy has 5 cans of vegetable juice in her refrigerator. Four of the cans each have 6 ounces of juice. Write an expression for the total ounces of juice Tracy has in her refrigerator. If the fifth can has 12 ounces, what is the total ounces of juice Tracy has?

_____

18 Brian says that the expression $8n + 2$ is equal to 83 when $n = 1$. Explain why Brian's answer is incorrect.

_____

_____

Read the problem below. Then continue exploring ways to write and evaluate expressions with variables.

Last year, the Speedster Bicycle Company held a bicycle design contest and awarded a cash prize. This year, the contest prize is $20 less than three times last year's prize. Evan and Gina win this year's contest and split the prize money evenly between them.

● Write an expression to show how much prize money Evan wins.

● If last year's prize was $50, how much prize money does Evan win?

Picture It

You can draw a picture to help you understand the problem.

You can represent the prize money as envelopes and draw a line to show Evan's half.

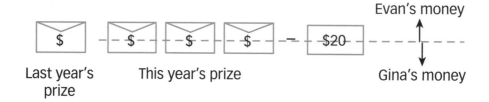

Last year's prize   This year's prize   Evan's money / Gina's money

Model It

You can use words to help you solve the problem.

The contest prize is $20 less than three times last year's prize.

The phrase *less than* tells you the expression representing this year's prize money will have this overall "shape."

First amount	–	Second amount

Evan gets half of this year's prize.

The phrase *half of* tells you this year's prize money is divided by 2. The expression representing Evan's share of this year's prize money will have this overall "shape."

First amount	–	Second amount

2

Connect It

Now you will solve the problem from the previous page using the picture and model.

19 Look at Model It on the previous page. This year's prize is "$20 less than" another amount. Will 20 be the first amount or the second amount? Explain.

_____

20 Explain how to write an expression for "three times last year's prize."

_____

21 Write an expression for "$20 less than three times last year's prize." _____

22 Chandler writes the expression $\frac{1}{2}(3x - 20)$ to represent Evan's winnings. Is she correct? Explain.

_____

23 Explain how you can find how much money Evan wins if last year's prize was $50.

_____

_____

_____

Try It

Use what you just learned to solve this problem.

24 The price of one share of XYZ Inc.'s stock drops by $0.02 on Monday. On Tuesday, the price goes back up by $0.05.

Write an expression with three terms to show the change in price of XYZ stock.

_____

If one share of XYZ stock cost $34.18 at the start of business on Monday morning, what is the price of one share of XYZ stock at the close of business on Tuesday evening?

_____

Study the student model below. Then solve problems 25–27.

This student used a model to think about the terms and operations Then, the student wrote an expression and solved for h = 3.

Student Model

During a car trip, LaTasha drives 65 miles per hour for several hours. She stops for gasoline, and then drives 40 miles more.

Write an expression to show how many miles LaTasha drives in all. Use your expression to find how many miles she drives in all if she drives for 3 hours before stopping for gasoline.

Look at how you could show your work using a model.

Miles before stop	+	Miles after stop

Miles before stop is "65 miles per hour for several hours": 65*h*

Miles after stop is "40 miles more": 40

Total miles is 65*h* + 40; evaluate for *h* = 3.

65(3) + 40 = 195 + 40 = 235

Solution: ___65*h* + 40; LaTasha drives a total of 235 miles.___

💬**Pair/Share**

Are there any other expressions that would also be correct?

Finding $\frac{1}{3}$ of an amount is the same as dividing that amount by 3.

25 Georgia is 2 years younger than $\frac{1}{3}$ of her Aunt Mika's age. Write an expression that describes Georgia's age. How old is Georgia if her Aunt Mika is 27?

Show your work.

💬**Pair/Share**

Would the expression *m* − 20 always give Georgia's age correctly?

Solution: _____

26 Shane buys 3 books. Each book is the same price. He also must pay $0.35 tax on each book. Write an expression to show the total cost of the books. If the price of each book is $5.15, how much does Shane spend in all?

Show your work.

Solution: _____

The total cost of each book is its price plus tax.

◎Pair/Share

How many terms are in the expression you wrote? Explain how you know.

27 Christi alters a skirt. She cuts 7 inches off the bottom of the skirt and then adds a 5-inch ruffle to the skirt's remaining bottom edge. Which expression best represents the final length of the skirt?

A $2 - s$

B $2 + s$

C $s - 2$

D $s - 12$

Evan chose **D** as the correct answer. How did he get that answer?

_____

_____

_____

_____

I can draw a picture to help myself understand this problem.

◎Pair/Share

Talk about the problem and then write your answer together.

Solve the problems.

1   How many coefficients are in the expression $5x^3 - 2x^3 + 6x - 4$?

     A   1

     B   2

     C   3

     D   4

2   Mila's dog weighs 4 pounds more than 8 times the weight of Keiko's dog. Which expression could be used to find the weight of Mila's dog?

     A $8k + 4$

     B $4k + 8$

     C $4(8k)$

     D $4 + 8 + k$

3   Match the algebraic expression with its English meaning by writing the expression in the appropriate box. *Not all expressions will have a match.*

$5 - 2x$ $5x + y$ $x^2 - 5$ $5x - 2$ $(25x)^2$ $(5 - x)^2$ $2x - 5$ $5(x + y)$

"Five less than twice a number"	"Five times the sum of two numbers"	"The difference of 5 and a number, squared"

4   Which of these expressions equal 15 when $x = \dfrac{1}{2}$ and $y = 3$? Circle all that apply.

     A $4(2y - 4x) - 1$ **D** $xy + 3\dfrac{1}{2} + 20x$

     B $4x^2 + 2y^3 - 10$ **E** $\dfrac{9}{y} + 14x^2$

     C $4(x^2 + 1) + 2x + 3y$

5 Keenan gives Tisha half of his strawberries. Tisha keeps 4 of the strawberries she got from Keenan and gives the rest to Suvi.

Part A

Write an expression for the number of strawberries Tisha gives to Suvi. Use *k* for the number of strawberries Keenan started with.

Answer _____

Part B

Could Keenan have started with 6 strawberries? Use your expression to explain why or why not.

Show your work.

Answer _____

6 Jason paints $\frac{1}{4}$ of the area of his living room walls, *w*, on Monday. On Tuesday, he paints twice as much as he painted on Monday.

Part A

Write an expression to find the remaining unpainted area.

Show your work.

Answer _____

Part B

Jason's living room has 210 square feet of wall. How much wall is left to paint?

Show your work.

Answer _____

✓ **Self Check** *Go back and see what you can check off on the Self Check on page 143.*

Lesson 17   Part 1: Introduction 👥

Equivalent Expressions

In Lesson 16, you learned to read, write, and evaluate expressions with variables. Now, take a look at this problem.

> Write an expression that is equivalent to $(3 + 14) + 27$.

🔍 Explore It

Use the math you know to answer the question.

- Which two terms in $(3 + 14) + 27$ could you add to get a multiple of ten? _____

- Rewrite the expression so that these two terms are next to each other.

  _____

- Did rewriting the expression change its value? Explain.

  _____

  _____

- Rewrite the expression with parentheses to show that the two terms with the sum that is a multiple of 10 should be added first. _____

- Did rewriting the expression change its value? Explain.

  _____

  _____

- What is the common factor of the numbers in parentheses? _____

- Rewrite the expression so that it is a number plus the product of a number and a sum. _____

- Does rewriting the expression this way change its value? Which property of operations supports your answer?

  _____

- Explain why you might want to write an equivalent expression.

  _____

Find Out More

In the problem on the previous page, you applied properties of operations to an expression with all constant terms to create equivalent expressions.

$(3 + 14) + 27 = (14 + 3) + 27$ **Commutative property of addition**
Reordering the terms does not change the value of the expression.

$(14 + 3) + 27 = 14 + (3 + 27)$ **Associative property of addition**
Regrouping the terms does not change the value of the expression.

$14 + (3 + 27) = 14 + 3(1 + 9)$ **Distributive property**
Distributing the common factor does not change the value of the expression.

The same is true for expressions with variable terms. You can apply properties of operations to a variable expression to create equivalent variable expressions.

$(3x + 14) + 27 = (14 + 3x) + 27$ Commutative property of addition

$(14 + 3x) + 27 = 14 + (3x + 27)$ Associative property of addition

$14 + (3x + 27) = 14 + 3(x + 9)$ Distributive property

Reflect

1 Henry says that you can apply the commutative and associative properties to $5x + 10$ and get $10x + 5$. Is Henry correct? Explain.

_____

_____

_____

_____

_____

_____

_____

_____

Read the problem below. Then explore how to use properties of operations to write equivalent expressions with variables.

Jamie has 4 bags of apples. Ashley has 3 bags of apples. Each bag has the same number of apples in it.

Write an expression for the total number of apples. Then simplify it to create an equivalent expression.

🔍 **Picture It**

Draw a picture of the bags of apples.

Jamie

Ashley

🔍 **Model It**

Model the apples with math tiles.

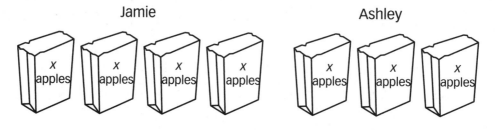

Connect It

Now solve the problem.

2 In both the Picture It and the Model It on the previous page, what does *x* represent?

_____

3 Write an expression for Jamie's total number of apples. _____ Write an expression

for Ashley's total number of apples. _____ Write an expression for the combined

total of Jamie's and Ashley's apples. _____

When two or more terms in a variable expression have the same variable factors, they
are called **like terms**. You can use the distributive property to simplify an expression
with like terms.

4 What is the common factor for each term in your expression from problem 3? _____

5 Distribute the common factor and simplify the expression.

_____

6 What does the simplified expression mean? _____

7 Explain how to simplify an expression with like terms, such as $6g + 5g$.

_____

Try It

**Use what you just learned about writing equivalent expressions to solve these
problems. Show your work on a separate sheet of paper.**

8 A school cafeteria has 30 boxes of Wheaty Squares cereal and 20 boxes of Mighty O's
cereal. Each box has the same number of ounces of cereal. Write an expression to
represent the total ounces of cereal. Then simplify it to create an equivalent expression.

_____

9 The inspector at a bottling plant checks 25 bottles. Two bottles do not pass
inspection. All the bottles hold the same number of milliliters of sports drink. Write an
expression for the milliliters of sports drink that pass inspection. Then simplify it to
create an equivalent expression.

_____

Read the problem below. Then continue exploring how to use properties of operations to write equivalent expressions with variables.

Javier creates a rectangular painting. The painting is 3 feet long and more than 2 feet wide. The expression $3(2 + x)$ represents the area of the painting.

Write an expression equivalent to $3(2 + x)$.

Model It

The multiplication expression $3(2 + x)$ means *three groups of* $2 + x$. Use math tiles to model three groups of $2 + x$.

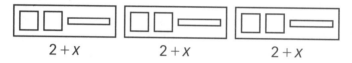

$2 + x$ $\qquad$ $2 + x$ $\qquad$ $2 + x$

Reorder and regroup the tiles.

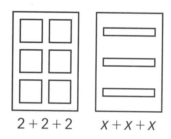

$2 + 2 + 2$ $\qquad$ $x + x + x$

Compare $3(2 + x)$ and $(2 + 2 + 2) + (x + x + x)$.

Picture It

Draw and label a picture of Javier's painting. Imagine dividing the painting into two smaller rectangles.

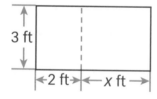

3 ft

←2 ft→|←— x ft —→

The area of the whole painting is $3(2 + x)$.

Connect It

Now solve the problem.

10 The expression $3(2 + x)$ is a product of the factors 3 and _____.

11 In the Model It, what expression is equivalent to $3(2 + x)$? Explain.

_____

_____

12 Look at the Picture It. Explain why the area of the whole picture is $3(2 + x)$.

_____

13 In the Picture It, the area of the left side of the rectangle is _____. The area
of the right side is _____. Write an expression for the area of the whole
painting: _____.

14 Compare $3(2 + x)$ to the equivalent expression in 13. What property did you apply?

_____

15 Simplify the expression from problem 14. _____

16 Is $3(2 + x)$ equivalent to your simplified expression? Explain.

_____

_____

Try It

**Use what you just learned about using the distributive property to write an
equivalent expression to solve these problems. Show your work on a separate
sheet of paper.**

17 Use the distributive property to write an expression that is equivalent to $5(2x - 1)$.

_____

18 Use the distributive property to write an expression that is equivalent to $18 + 24x$.

_____

Read the problem below. Then explore how to determine if expressions are equivalent.

Is $5h + 2h^2$ equivalent to $7h$? Explain.

Picture It

Imagine line segments that are h, $5h$, and $7h$ units long.

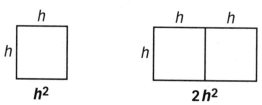

Imagine rectangles that are h^2 and $2h^2$ square units in area.

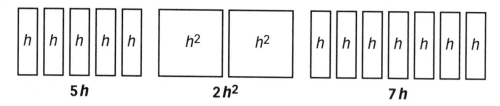

Model It

Use math tiles to model $5h$, $2h^2$, and $7h$.

Connect It

Now solve the problem.

19 Look at Picture It. If you combine the line that is $5h$ units long and the rectangle that is $2h^2$ units in area, do you get a figure that looks like the line that is $7h$ units long? _____

20 Look at Model It. If you put the tiles representing $5h$ together with the tiles representing $2h^2$, do you get a set of tiles that represents $7h$? _____

21 Richard says that $5h$ and $2h^2$ are like terms because they both have the variable h. Is Richard correct? Explain.

_____

_____

_____

22 Is $5h + 2h^2 = 7h$ a true statement? Substitute a value other than zero for h and evaluate $5h + 2h^2$ and $7h$ to support your answer.

_____

_____

23 Apply the distributive property to write an expression that is equivalent to $5h + 2h^2$. Show your work.

_____

_____

Try It

Use what you just learned to solve these problems. Show your work on a separate sheet of paper.

24 Are $3x + 6 + x$ and $2(2x + 3)$ equivalent expressions? Use substitution to check your answer.

_____

25 Are $8(w + 6)$ and $5 + 8w + 1$ equivalent expressions? Use substitution to check your answer.

_____

Study the student model below. Then solve problems 26–28.

Two expressions are equivalent if you can simplify one expression and get the other expression.

Are $y + 2y - 3$ and $3(y - 1)$ equivalent expressions? Explain.

Look at how you can apply the properties of operations to show your answer.

$y + 2y - 3 = y(1 + 2) - 3$
$\quad\quad\quad\quad\quad = 3y - 3$
$\quad\quad\quad\quad\quad = 3(y - 1)$

Solution: __Yes; I can apply the properties of operations to__

$y + 2y - 3$ without changing its value and get $3(y - 1)$. If I let

$y = 2$, $y + 2y - 3 = 2 + 2(2) - 3 = 2 + 4 - 3 = 6 - 3 = 3$

and $3(y - 1) = 3(2 - 1) = 3(1) = 3$. Since $3 = 3$, I know

$y + 2y - 3 = 3(y - 1)$.

💬 Pair/Share

Which property of operations allows you to combine like terms without changing the value of an expression?

26 Simplify $6x^3 + 6x^2 + 6x$ to get an equivalent expression. Label any properties of operations that you use.

Show your work.

If the terms of an expression have a common factor, you can apply the distributive property to simplify the expression.

💬 Pair/Share

Are $6x^3$ and $6x^2$ like terms? Why or why not?

Solution: _____

27 Dalia's living room is 12 feet long and 10 feet wide. Her dining room is also 10 feet wide. Write two equivalent expressions that each represent the combined area of the two rooms.

Show your work.

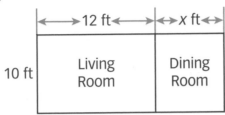

Solution: _____

28 Which expression is equivalent to $2 + 3n + 2 + 9n$?

A $16n$

B $3n + 8$

C $4(3n + 1)$

D $4(3n + 4)$

Anya chose **D** as the correct answer. How did she get that answer?

_____

_____

_____

_____

Draw and label a picture to help you organize the given information.

🗨 **Pair/Share**

How could you show that the two expressions are equivalent?

Combine like terms and apply properties of operations to simplify an expression.

🗨 **Pair/Share**

How could Anya check her answer?

Solve the problems.

1   The expression $0.25(2d + 1)$ represents the fines per day, *d,* for overdue books. Which expression is equivalent to $0.25(2d + 1)$?

   A $0.252d + 1$

   B $0.50d + 0.25$

   C $2d + 0.25$

   D $0.50d + 1$

2   A game company makes a board game that comes with 2 dice and a card game that comes with 3 dice. Which expression shows the total number of dice in *b* boxes of the board game and *b* boxes of the card game?

   A $5b$

   B $5(2b)$

   C $5 + b$

   D $2b + 3$

3   Look at the equations below. Choose True or False for each equation.

   A $f + f + f = 3f$ ☐ True   ☐ False

   B $4 \times n \times n \times n \times n = 4n^4$ ☐ True   ☐ False

   C $10h - 10 = 10 - 10h$ ☐ True   ☐ False

   D $x^2 + 3v = (x + x) + v \times v \times v$ ☐ True   ☐ False

   E $6 \times (2 + 7) = (6 \times 2) + 7$ ☐ True   ☐ False

4 Look at each expression below. Is it equivalent to $42x - 56y$? Select Yes or No for expressions A–D.

A $7(6x - 8y)$ ☐ Yes   ☐ No

B $40(2x - 16y)$ ☐ Yes   ☐ No

C $14(x + 2x + 7y - 3y)$ ☐ Yes   ☐ No

D $42(x + 14y)$ ☐ Yes   ☐ No

5 Taylor writes an expression with 5 terms. All 5 terms are like terms. How many terms are in the equivalent expression with the *least* number of terms? Explain.

_____

_____

_____

_____

_____

6 Kari uses substitution to decide whether $x^2 + x$ is equivalent to $x(2x + 1)$. She says the expressions are equivalent because they have the same value when $x = 0$. Is Kari correct? Explain.

_____

_____

_____

_____

_____

✓ **Self Check**   *Go back and see what you can check off on the Self Check on page 143.*

Understand Solutions to Equations

What does it mean to solve an equation?

Have you ever seen a pan balance? You put objects in both pans. If the objects' weights are the same, the pans hang evenly.

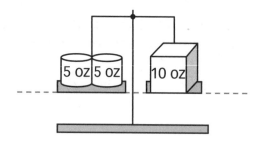

An equation is like a pan balance. A pan balance tells you two weights are equivalent. An equation tells you two expressions are equivalent.

Think   Solving an equation is like making the pans of a balance hang evenly.

Imagine a pan balance like the one below.

> **Look at the picture. Circle the weights that must combine to equal 6 ounces.**

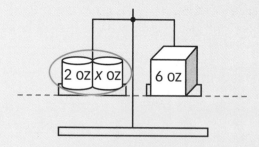

The pans are hanging evenly, so the total weight in each pan is the same. The pan on the right holds 6 ounces. The pan on the left must also hold 6 ounces.

How much weight do you have to add to 2 ounces to get a total of 6 ounces? 2 ounces and 4 ounces together are a total of 6 ounces. Therefore, the unknown weight, x, must be 4 ounces.

Write an expression for the weight in the right-side pan: 6.

An **equation** is a statement that tells you two expressions are equivalent.

$2 + x = 6$ is an equation.

"Solve the equation" means you need to find the value of the variable that will make the expression $2 + x$ equivalent to 6.

What number can you add to 2 to get 6?

Write an expression for the weight in the left-side pan: $2 + x$.

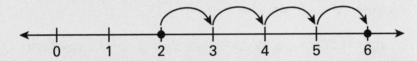

Adding 4 to 2 gives a total of 6. So, the solution of $2 + x = 6$ is that x must be equal to 4.

✏️ **Reflect**

1 What would the balance look like if you replace the unknown weight with an 8-ounce weight?

_____

_____

Explain why the solution of $2 + x = 6$ cannot be that x is equal to 8.

_____

_____

Explore It

Explore writing and solving equations with the problem below.

Andres buys 3 boxes of markers. Each box has the same number of markers. Andres now has 15 markers. Write and solve an equation to find how many markers are in one box.

2 Choose a variable to represent the number of markers in one box. _____

3 Write an expression to describe the total markers in 3 boxes. _____

4 How many markers does Andres have in all? _____

5 Write an equation that compares your answers from problems 3 and 4. _____

Use a bar model to help you solve the equation.

6 Draw a bar model to represent your equation from problem 5.

7 What number could you multiply by 3 to get 15? _____

8 What is the solution to your equation? _____

9 How many markers are in each box? _____

Now try these two problems.

10 At noon the temperature on Jessica's porch was 75° F. Then the temperature dropped *d* degrees. By midnight, the temperature on the porch was 63° F. Write an equation with an expression equivalent to the temperature at midnight. _____

11 By how many degrees did the temperature drop between noon and midnight? What is the solution to your equation?

_____

_____

Talk About It

Solve the problem below as a group.

> Marta earns $12.50 from babysitting, and then spends some of her earnings on a new book. She has $8.00 of her earnings left. Write and solve an equation to find the cost of the book.

12 What is the unknown amount? _____ Choose a variable to

represent it. _____

13 Could the value of the variable be greater than $12.50? Explain.

_____

_____

14 Write an equation with an expression equivalent to $8.00. _____

15 Draw a number line from 7.5 to 13.5.

16 What number can you subtract from 12.5 to get 8? _____

17 What is the solution of your equation? _____

18 What is the cost of the book? _____

Try It Another Way

Explore using math tiles to solve an equation.

19 Write your equation from problem 14. _____

20 Use math tiles to represent the equation.

21 What amount can you subtract from $12.50 to get $8.00? _____

22 What is the cost of the book? _____

Connect It

Talk through these problems as a class, then write your answers below.

23 **Analyze:** Explain why the solution to $3r = 2$ must be less than 1.

_____

_____

24 **Illustrate:** Use a bar model to illustrate the equation $20 - x = 6$. Explain how you would solve the equation.

_____

_____

25 **Create:** Write a real-world problem that you could represent with the equation $3 + x = 10$. Solve the equation to find the answer to your problem.

_____

_____

_____

_____

🔍 **Put It Together**

26 Imagine you have a pan balance. The left pan holds a bag with an unknown number of identical blocks and 10 more blocks you can see. Assume the bag itself has no weight. The other pan is empty.

A Draw a picture of what the balance would look like in this situation.

B Suppose you put 13 identical blocks in the right-side pan and this makes the pans hang evenly. Draw a picture of the balance. What equation does this represent?

_____

C Suppose you take 10 blocks out of each pan. Draw a picture of the balance. What does the number of blocks in the right-side pan tell you? Explain how you know.

_____

_____

_____

_____

_____

_____

183

You have seen that an equation is a statement that states two expressions are equivalent. In Lesson 18 you learned what it means to solve an equation. Take a look at this problem.

The diagram to the right shows a pan balance holding 10 blocks and a bag with an unknown number of blocks. The pans hang evenly. How many blocks are in the bag?

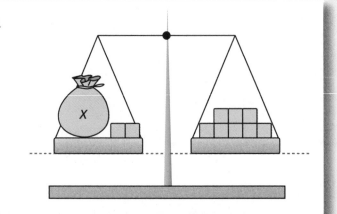

🔍 Explore It

Use the math you know to answer the question.

🔲 What does the letter *x* represent? _____

🔲 How many blocks are in the right-side pan?_____

🔲 Write an expression for the number of blocks in the left-side pan. _____

🔲 What will you need to do to get the bag by itself on the left side?

_____

🔲 Then, what must you also do to keep the pans hanging evenly?

_____

Explain how you could find the number of blocks in the bag.

_____

_____

_____

Find Out More

To find the number of blocks in the bag, you had to do two things.

First: Get the bag with the unknown number of blocks by itself on one side of the balance. You did this by taking away 2 blocks from the pan with the bag.

Second: Keep the pans hanging evenly. You did this by also taking away 2 blocks from the other pan.

The pan balance, blocks, and bag represent the equation $x + 2 = 8$.

To solve the equation $x + 2 = 8$, you have to do two things.

First: Get the variable x by itself on one side of the equal sign. Another way to say this is you need to *isolate the variable*.

Second: Keep the two expressions equivalent to each other. Another way to say this is you need to keep the equation *balanced*.

How do you isolate the variable x in the equation $x + 2 = 8$? Use *inverse operations*. Inverse operations are operations that "undo" each other. Addition and subtraction are inverse operations. Since the expression $x + 2$ has 2 being added to x, you can isolate x by subtracting 2 from $x + 2$.

How do you keep the equation balanced after isolating x? Subtract 2 from the other side of the equation.

$$\text{isolate the variable} \longrightarrow x + 2 = 8$$
$$x + 2 - 2 = 8 - 2 \longleftarrow \text{balance the equation}$$
$$x + (2 - 2) = 8 - 2$$
$$x + 0 = 6$$
$$x = 6$$

Reflect

1 Write an equation for which subtracting 5 from an expression would isolate the variable.

_____

Read the problem below. Then explore how to solve a subtraction equation.

> Suppose you have a bag with an unknown number of blocks and you take 3 blocks
> out of the bag. Then you put the bag in one pan of a pan balance. It takes 7 blocks
> in the other pan to make the pans hang evenly. How many blocks were in the bag
> before you took 3 out?

🔍 Picture It

Draw the balance, bag, and blocks.

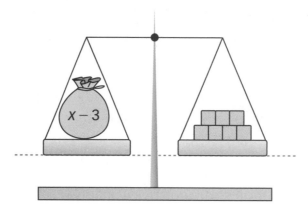

The label on the bag means "the bag has 3 less than some number of blocks in it."

🔍 Solve It

Write an expression for the number of blocks in each pan.

number of blocks in left-side pan: $x - 3$
number of blocks in right-side pan: 7

Since the pans are hanging evenly, you know there is the same number of blocks in each
pan. Write an equation to show the expressions are equivalent.

number of blocks in left-side pan = number of blocks in right-side pan

$$x - 3 = 7$$

Connect It

Now use inverse operations to solve the problem.

2 Look at Solve It on the previous page. If you solve the equation $x - 3 = 7$, what information will you have? _____

3 What is the operation in the expression $x - 3$? _____

4 What is the inverse of this operation? _____

5 How can you isolate the variable in $x - 3 = 7$? _____

6 When you isolate the variable, what must you do to keep the equation balanced?

_____

7 Solve $x - 3 = 7$.

$$x - 3 = 7$$

isolate the variable $x - 3 \underline{\quad} = 7 \underline{\quad}$ balance the equation

$$x \underline{\quad} = \underline{\quad}$$

$$x = \underline{\quad}$$

8 How many blocks were in the bag before you took 3 out? _____

Try It

Use what you just learned to solve these problems. Show your work.

9 Solve $x + 5 = 15$.

10 Solve $x - 9 = 8$.

Read the problem below. Then explore how to solve a multiplication equation.

Delia puts two bags of blocks in the left-side pan of a balance. Each bag has the same number of blocks. After she adds 10 blocks to the right-side pan, the pans hang evenly. How many blocks are in 1 bag?

🔍 **Picture It**

Draw the balance, bags, and blocks.

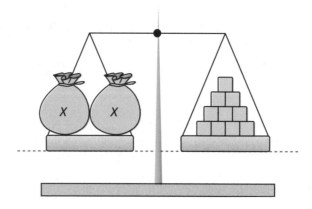

The 2 bags together have a total of 10 blocks.

🔍 **Solve It**

Write an expression for the number of blocks in each pan.

number of blocks in left-side pan: 2x
number of blocks in right-side pan: 10

Since the pans are hanging evenly, you know there is the same number of blocks in each pan. Write an equation showing the expressions are equivalent.

number of blocks in left-side pan = number of blocks in right-side pan

$$2x = 10$$

Connect It

Now use inverse operations to solve the problem.

11 Look at Solve It on the previous page. What do you need to do to find the number of blocks in 1 bag? _____

12 The expression $2x$ is a multiplication expression. It tells you to combine 2 equal groups of x blocks each. What is the "opposite" of combining two equal groups of blocks.

_____

13 What operation is the inverse of multiplication? _____

14 How can you isolate the variable in $2x = 10$? _____

15 When you isolate the variable, what must you do to balance the equation?

_____

16 Write numbers inside the boxes to solve $2x = 10$.

$$2x = 10$$

isolate the variable $\dfrac{2x}{\Box} = \dfrac{10}{\Box}$ balance the equation

$$x = 5$$

17 How many blocks are in 1 bag? _____

18 How could you check your solution? _____

_____

Try It

Use what you just learned to solve this problem. Show your work.

19 Solve $7x = 21$.

Read the problem below. Then explore how to write and solve an equation based on a real-world situation.

> Rita sells 6 tickets for a school fundraiser. The total price of the 6 tickets is $84.
> What is the price of 1 ticket?

Model It

Create a bar model to represent the 6 tickets and the total price. Let *t* be the price of 1 ticket.

t	*t*	*t*	*t*	*t*	*t*

$\longleftarrow$ $84 $\longrightarrow$

The top bar represents $84, the total price of the 6 tickets.

The bottom bar represents the expression 6*t*, the total price of the 6 tickets Rita sells.

The bars are the same length, so 6*t* = 84.

Solve It

Let the price of each ticket be *t* dollars. Write a sentence describing two amounts in the problem that are equivalent. Then, translate your sentence into math symbols.

The number of tickets times the price per ticket equals the total price of the tickets.

$$6 \qquad \bullet \qquad t \qquad = \qquad 84$$

Write an equation.

6*t* = 84.

Solve this equation to find *t*, the price of 1 ticket.

🔍 Connect It

Now use inverse operations to solve the problem.

20 Look at Solve It on the previous page. What is the operation in the equation $6t = 84$?

_____

21 What is the inverse of this operation?

_____

22 What is the first step to solve the equation?

_____

23 What must you do to keep the equation balanced?

_____

24 Write numbers inside the boxes to solve $6t = 84$.

$$6t = 84$$

isolate the variable $\quad \dfrac{6t}{\Box} = \dfrac{84}{\Box} \quad$ balance the equation

$$t = 14$$

25 What is the price of 1 ticket? _____

26 Explain how you know what step to take to solve an equation.

_____

_____

_____

✏️ Try It

Use what you just learned to solve this problem. Show your work on a separate sheet of paper.

27 Marie drives 35 miles per hour and travels a total of 105 miles. For how many hours does Marie drive?

_____

Study the student model below. Then solve problems 28–30.

The student wrote an equation then used an inverse operation to solve the problem.

Amanda's age is William's age divided by 2. If Amanda is 12 years old, how old is William?

Look at how you could solve this problem.

Write a sentence describing two amounts in the problem that are equivalent. Then, translate your sentence into math symbols and write an equation.

Amanda's age is William's age divided by 2.

$$12 \qquad = \qquad \frac{w}{2}$$

The equation is $12 = \frac{w}{2}$.

$$12 = 2w$$
$$2 \cdot 12 = 2 \cdot \frac{w}{2}$$
$$24 = w$$

Solution: <u>**William is 24 years old.**</u>

💬 Pair/Share

How do you know your solution is correct?

Before you begin writing, ask yourself, "Should the solution be less than or greater than $25?"

28 Ray and Hunter sell newspapers after school. Ray earns $11 more than Hunter. If Ray earns $25, how much money does Hunter earn?

Show your work.

💬 Pair/Share

How could you use a bar model to help solve this problem?

Solution: _____

29 Nina has 2 cups of flour. However, this is only $\frac{1}{4}$ of the amount of flour that she needs for a bread recipe. How many cups of flour does the recipe call for?

Show your work.

What inverse operation will isolate the variable?

Solution: _____

🗨**Pair/Share**

Can you write a different equation to describe this situation?

30 Tara and Julia run a race. Julia takes 42 seconds to run the race. She is 7 seconds faster than Tara. How many seconds does Tara take?

A 6 seconds

B 35 seconds

C 49 seconds

D 294 seconds

Nolan chose **B** as the correct answer. How did he get that answer?

_____

_____

Which girl takes the least amount of time to finish the race?

🗨**Pair/Share**

Talk about the problem and then write your answer together.

Solve the problems.

1 Solve the following equation for a.

$$a - 32 = 47$$

A $a = 15$

B $a = 47$

C $a = 64$

D $a = 79$

2 Ali reads a story and a play. The play has 165 pages, which is 5 times as many pages as the story. Which equation could you use to find s, the number of pages in the story?

A $\frac{1}{5}s = 165$

B $6x - 1$

C $5s = 165$

D $165s = 5$

3 Caroline charges $15 per hour babysitting. Let h represent the number of hours she babysits and E represent how much she earns. Choose True or False for each statement.

A $h + 15 = E$ is the equation that represents how much Caroline earns after h hours. ☐ True ☐ False

B If Caroline babysits for 5 hours, she earns $20. ☐ True ☐ False

C $15h = E$ is the equation that represents how much Caroline earns after h hours. ☐ True ☐ False

D If Caroline earned $52.50, then she babysat for $3\frac{1}{2}$ hours. ☐ True ☐ False

E $75f$ represents how much Caroline makes after f number of days babysitting 5 hours a day. ☐ True ☐ False

4 Which scenario could be represented by the following expression? Circle all that apply.

$48 + 2x$

A Sara's phone contract costs her $48 per month, but she pays an additional $2 for every minute she goes over her allotted minutes.

B A fast food restaurant expects to use 48 eggs per day plus an additional 2 eggs for every customer coming in for breakfast.

C A florist began the day with 48 roses and sold approximately 2 roses per hour.

D The entrance fee to the amusement park is $48 plus $2 for each ticket purchased for the rides.

5 A builder has built $\frac{1}{6}$ of the floors of a new skyscraper. If the builder has built 13 floors, how many floors will the skyscraper have when it is finished? Write and solve an equation to find the answer.

6 Big-Box brand computers have $\frac{1}{4}$ of the gigabytes of RAM that Zap brand computers have. A Big-Box computer has 20 gigabytes of RAM. Maia and Jada each write an equation to find how many gigabytes of RAM a Zap computer has. Is one, both, or neither girl correct? Solve each correct equation.

Maia: $20 = \frac{1}{4}z$　　　Jada: $20 = \frac{z}{4}$

✓ **Self Check** *Go back and see what you can check off on the Self Check on page 143.*

Lesson 20   Part 1: Introduction 👥

Solving Inequalities

You've learned how to replace values for variables into equations to see if they are true. Take a look at this problem.

> A grocery store is giving a reusable bag to every person who donates more than $5 to charity. Let x equal the amount that a person donates. Use words and symbols to solve all of the following problems about this situation.

🔍 Explore It

Use the math you already know to solve these problems.

▪ Ella donates $5.50. Will she get a bag? Explain how you know.

_____

▪ Daniel donates $5. Will he get a bag? Explain how you know.

_____

▪ Courtney donates $1.25. Will she get a bag? Explain how you know.

_____

▪ Name 2 other amounts people could contribute and get a bag.

_____

▪ To get a bag, are the amounts greater than or less than $5?

_____

▪ Use the symbols $>$ or $<$ to show x is greater than $5.

_____

▪ Explain how you know when any person should receive a free bag.

_____

_____

Find Out More

A sentence such as $x > 5$ is called an **inequality**. On the previous page you identified values for x that make $x > 5$ true, like 5.50 or 10, but there are too many possible values for x to be counted. Unlike an equation that has one solution, an inequality has infinitely many solutions.

Here are some symbols and words to describe an inequality:

>	≥	<	≤
• is more than • is greater than • above	• greater than or equal to • at least • no less than • minimum	• is less than • below	• less than or equal to • at most • no more than • no greater than • maximum
x is greater than 5 $x > 5$	x is at least 5 $x \geq 5$	x is below 5 $x < 5$	x is at most 5 $x \leq 5$

Reflect

1 Explain the difference between an equation, like $x = 5$, and an inequality, like $x \geq 5$.

_____

_____

_____

Read the problem below. Then explore how to write and solve an inequality.

When the temperature drops below 15°C in a building, the furnace turns on. At what temperatures will the heater turn on? Write an inequality to represent this situation, and graph the solution on a number line.

Model It

You can use words and symbols to represent the problem.

Let x equal the temperature in a building. When x is less than 15, the heater turns on.

$x < 15$

Graph It

You can graph the inequality on a number line to show all solutions.

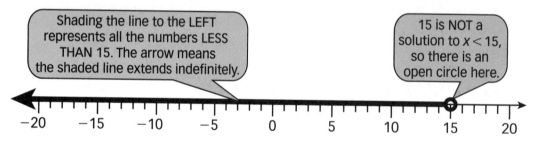

Shading the line to the LEFT represents all the numbers LESS THAN 15. The arrow means the shaded line extends indefinitely.

15 is NOT a solution to $x < 15$, so there is an open circle here.

A closed or shaded circle on the above graph would show the solutions for $x \leq 15$.

Check It

You can substitute values for x to check your solution.

The graph shows that −5°C is a possible solution. You can replace x with −5 to check.

$x < 15$

$-5 < 15$ TRUE

The graph shows that 16°C is not a solution. You can replace x with 16 to check.

$16 < 15$ FALSE

Connect It

Now you will solve the problem using the model and graph.

2 What words in the problem help you know which inequality symbol to use?

_____

3 Look at the graph. Why is there an open circle at 15? What does it mean?

_____

_____

4 Explain the meaning of the shaded line and arrow to the left of 15.

_____

_____

5 Would the heater turn on if the temperature was 2.5°C? Explain how you know.

_____

6 Suppose the heater turns on when the temperature is at 15°C or below.

Write an inequality for this new situation. _____

Graph the solution on the number line below.

7 Explain when to use an open or closed circle when graphing an inequality.

_____

_____

Try It

Use what you just learned about graphing inequalities to solve this problem.

8 This graph shows the solution of what inequality? _____

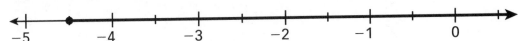

Read the problem below. Then explore how to write and solve an inequality.

Cooper spent at least $25 at a music concert. What are some possible amounts of money Cooper could have spent? Write an inequality to represent the amount of money Cooper spent, and graph the solution on a number line.

Model It

You can use words and symbols to represent this problem.

The amount Cooper spent, x, is greater than or equal to $25.

$$x \geq 25$$

Another way to think about this problem is that $25 is less than or equal to the amount Cooper spent, so $25 \leq x$.

Model It

You can graph the inequality on a number line to solve the problem.

Check It

You can substitute values for x to check your solution.

The graph shows that $25.50 is a possible solution. You can replace x with 25.5 to check.

$$x \geq 25$$

$$25.5 \geq 25 \qquad\qquad \text{TRUE}$$

The graph shows that $30 is a possible solution. You can replace x with 30 to check.

$$25 \leq x$$

$$25 \leq 30 \qquad\qquad \text{TRUE}$$

Connect It

Now you will solve the problem using the model and graph.

9 Explain how $x \geq 25$ and $25 \leq x$ both represent the amount Cooper spent at the concert.

_____

_____

10 Look at the graph of $x \geq 25$. What does the closed circle at 25 mean?

_____

11 What is a possible amount of money Cooper could have spent? Check your solution.

_____

12 How would the inequality be different if the problem said that Cooper spent more than $25? Write and graph the inequality on the number line below.

_____

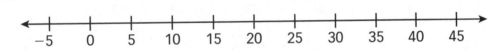

13 Explain how a shaded line means that fractions, decimals, and numbers not labeled on a number line can be part of the solution to an inequality.

_____

_____

Try It

Use what you just learned about writing and graphing inequalities to solve this problem.

14 Some sources say that Earth's atmosphere does not exist above $30\frac{1}{2}$ km. Write an

inequality to represent this situation. _____

Now graph the solution on the number line below.

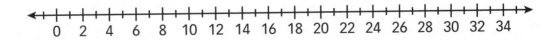

Study the student model below. Then solve problems 15–17.

The student replaced the variable, x, with a value to see if the inequality was true.

Student Model

Which of the following values is not a solution of $x - 4 < 15$?

$$0, \ 19, \ 18.9, \ 15\tfrac{1}{4}$$

Look at how you can show your work using a model.

$0 - 4 < 15$
$-4 < 15$ **TRUE**

$19 - 4 < 15$
$15 < 15$ **FALSE**

$18.9 - 4 < 15$
$14.9 < 15$ **TRUE**

$15\tfrac{1}{4} - 4 < 15$

$11\tfrac{1}{4} < 15$ **TRUE**

Solution: ___19 is not a solution of $x - 4 < 15$___

Pair/Share

How could you justify your answer by graphing the solution on a number line?

15 Which of the following values is a solution of $12.6 \leq 3x$?

$$4, \ 4.2, \ 3, \ 10$$

Show your work.

When you replace the x with each value, does that value make the inequality true or false?

Pair/Share

How is this problem similar to and different from the student model?

Solution: _____

16 Algae cannot survive at depths greater than 300 meters below sea level. The inequality to represent this situation is $x \leq -300$. Graph the solution on a number line.

Show your work.

Will your graph have an open or a closed circle?

Solution:

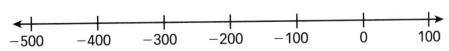

$$-500 \quad -400 \quad -300 \quad -200 \quad -100 \quad 0 \quad 100$$

Pair/Share

How could you use substitution to check your graph?

17 Which inequality represents the situation: Hailey has at most $500 in her bank account?

A $x > 500$

B $x \geq 500$

C $x < 500$

D $x \leq 500$

Tessa chose **C** as the correct answer. How did she get that answer?

Does "at most 500" include 500 as a possible solution?

_____

_____

_____

_____

Pair/Share

What are some words that help you know when to use < and when to use ≤?

Solve the problems.

1   Which is a correct graph of $x \leq -1\frac{1}{4}$?

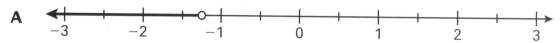

A

B

C

D

2   Mark cannot read traffic signs that are more than 50 meters away. Which inequality represents distances at which Mark cannot read signs?

A $x > 50$

B $x \geq 50$

C $x < 50$

D $x \leq 50$

3   Look at the inequality $5x + 1 \geq 35$. Choose True or False for each statement.

A   100 is not a solution because it is much greater than 35.   ☐ True   ☐ False

B   7.04 cannot be a solution because only whole numbers can be solutions.   ☐ True   ☐ False

C $6\frac{4}{5}$ is not a solution because the expression on the left side cannot equal 35.   ☐ True   ☐ False

D   There are an infinite number of solutions.   ☐ True   ☐ False

E   34 is not a solution because it is less than 35.   ☐ True   ☐ False

4 Which inequality does this graph represent?

Insert the appropriate inequality symbol to complete the statement.

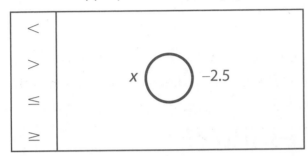

$<$

$>$

$\leq$

$\geq$

x ◯ -2.5

5 Eric has practiced more than 40 hours with his band.

Write an inequality to express this situation. _____

On the graph below, graph Eric's situation.

6 Judah's family wants to ride the bumper boats at a water park.

- There are 4 children (c) and 2 adults (a) in Judah's family.
- The boats are safe if $40c + 120a \leq 500$.

Can Judah's family ride the bumper boats safely? Explain.

Show your work.

Answer _____

✓ **Self Check** *Go back and see what you can check off on the Self Check on page 143.*

Lesson 21   Part 1: Introduction 👥

Dependent and Independent Variables

You've learned how to use variables to describe situations. Take a look at this problem.

Tickets for the school musical are $8 per ticket. This table shows the total cost, c, for a certain number of tickets, t. Complete the table and describe the relationship between the total cost and tickets purchased.

Tickets, t	Total cost, c
1	$8
2	$16
3	
4	
5	$40

🔍 Explore It

Use the math you already know to solve this problem.

- What are the two quantities in this situation?

  _____

- If you know the number of tickets, you can find the total cost. Which quantity depends on the other?

  _____

- Find the total cost for 3 tickets and 4 tickets.

  _____

- Use words to explain the relationship between tickets and total cost.

  _____

- Explain how you found the total cost for 3 tickets and 4 tickets.

  _____

  _____

Find Out More

In the problem on the previous page, the total cost of tickets, c, depends on how many tickets are purchased, t. An equation representing the relationship between t and c looks like this:

$$c = 8t$$

The total cost equals 8 times the number of tickets purchased.

The number of tickets purchased, t, is the **independent variable**. The total cost, c, is the **dependent variable**. The total cost depends on the number of tickets purchased.

You can use the equation to find the total cost of any number of tickets. For example, if you bought 20 tickets, replacing t with 20 and solving for c will show the total cost.

$c = 8t$
$c = 8 \cdot 20$
$c = \$160$

20 tickets cost $160.

Reflect

1 Lunch costs $2.25 per day. An equation showing the relationship between the number of days, d, and the total cost of lunch, c, is $c = 2.25d$. What is the dependent variable? Explain how you know this.

_____

_____

_____

_____

Read the problem below. Then explore how to represent the relationship between variables with a table, an equation, and a graph.

Lincoln's school is selling candles to raise money for a new track. Each candle is $20. The table shows the relationship between the number of candles sold, c, and money raised, m. Use the table to write an equation and draw a graph to represent this problem.

Number of candles sold, c	0	1	2	3	4	5
Amount of money raised, m ($)	0	20	40	60	80	100

Model It

You can use words and an equation to represent this problem.

An equation with two variables can represent the relationship between c and m.

money raised **equals** cost of each candle **times** number of candles

$$m \quad = \quad 20 \quad \cdot \quad c$$

Graph It

You can draw a graph to represent this problem.

You can think of c and m as x- and y-coordinates and write ordered pairs to graph the equation.

(0, 0), (1, 20), (2, 40), (3, 60), (4, 80), and (5, 100)

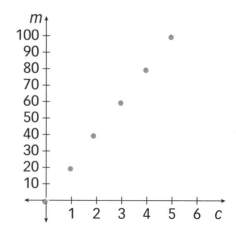

These points show solutions to the equation $m = 20c$.

✎ Connect It

Now you will explain how the table, the equation, and the graph are related.

2 Which value is the dependent variable? Which is the independent variable? Explain.

_____

_____

_____

3 Look at the graph. How does the point (2, 40) relate to the equation and table?

_____

_____

_____

4 Use the equation to explain how much money Lincoln raised if he sold 9 candles.

_____

_____

_____

5 What coordinates on the graph would show how much money Lincoln raised if he sold 9 candles? Explain.

_____

_____

_____

✏ Try It

Use what you just learned about representing problems with a graph to answer this question.

6 Explain how the coordinates of a point on a graph relate to the dependent and independent variables of an equation.

_____

_____

_____

L21: Dependent and Independent Variables　　　　　　　　　　　　　　　　**209**

Read the problem below. Then explore how to represent a problem with an equation, a table, and a graph.

It costs $6 to enter a skating rink and $2.50/hour to rent skates. The equation below represents the total cost, *c*, to skate and rent skates for a certain amount of time, *t*.

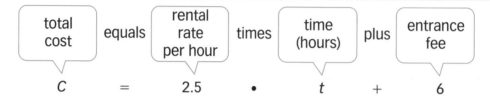

| total cost | equals | rental rate per hour | times | time (hours) | plus | entrance fee |
| c | = | 2.5 | • | t | + | 6 |

Show the relationship between *c* and *t* using a table and graph.

Model It

You can use a table to understand this problem.

Time, *t* (hours)	2.5*t* + 6	Total cost, *c* ($)
1	2.5 (1) + 6	8.5
2	2.5 (2) + 6	11
3	2.5 (3) + 6	13.5
4	2.5 (4) + 6	16

Graph It

You can draw a graph to represent this problem.

You can write ordered pairs from the table and graph them on a coordinate plane.

(1, 8.5), (2, 11), (3, 13.5), (4, 16)

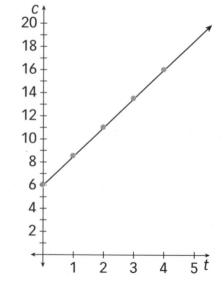

Connecting the points with a line shows all the solutions of $c = 2.5t + 6$.

Connect It

Now you will explain how the table and graph relate to the equation.

7 Which value is the dependent variable? Which is the independent variable? Explain.

_____

_____

8 Use the equation to explain the total amount Melissa pays if she skates for 5 hours.

_____

9 How would you represent $t = 5$ on the table? On the graph? Explain.

_____

_____

10 Describe two ways to represent the total cost of skating for half an hour.

_____

_____

11 Given any equation with two variables, explain how to draw a table and a graph.

_____

_____

_____

_____

Try It

Use what you just learned about representing problems with an equation.

12 A lodge rents snowboards for $40/day plus a $20 flat fee for safety gear. Write an equation to represent the relationship between total cost, c, and number of days renting a snowboard, d.

_____

Study the student model below. Then solve problems 13–15.

Given the value of s, the student used the equation to solve for the value of m.

Taylor's computer can download movies at a rate of 10.2 megabytes per minute.

A Write an equation to show the relationship between the number of minutes, *m*, it takes to download a certain sized movie, *s*.

B Use your equation to explain how long it takes Taylor's computer to download a movie that is 52.02 megabytes.

Look at how you can show your work using a model.

A $s = 10.2m$ or $\frac{s}{10.2} = m$

B $s = 52.02$ megabytes, so I replace *s* in the equation with 52.02.

$\frac{52.02}{10.2} = 5.1$ minutes

$$
\begin{array}{r}
5.1 \\
102\overline{)520.2} \\
510 \\
\hline
10.2 \\
10.2 \\
\hline
0
\end{array}
$$

💬**Pair/Share**

What is the dependent variable? What is the independent variable?

Which value depends on another value?

13 Justin drove at a steady speed of 60 miles/hour. Write an equation to represent the relationship between the total distance Justin drove, *d*, in a certain amount of time, *t*. Which value is the dependent variable? Which is the independent variable? Explain.

Show your work.

💬**Pair/Share**

How far does Justin travel in 1 hour? Half an hour? 2 hours?

Solution: _____

_____

_____

14 Mary and Will rent a tandem bike for $10/hr. Which value is the dependent variable? Which is the independent variable? Write an equation to represent the relationship between the number of hours, *h*, and the total cost, *c*.

Show your work.

How does knowing the dependent variable and the independent variable help you write an equation?

Solution: _____

_____

_____

🗨 **Pair/Share**

What would a table and graph of this equation look like?

15 Which ordered pair is not included in a graph of $y = 2x + 5$?

A (0, 0)

B (1, 7)

C (0.5, 6)

D (2, 9)

David chose **A** as the correct answer. How did he get that answer?

_____

_____

_____

What will y equal if x = 0? 1? 0.5? 2?

🗨 **Pair/Share**

When might the point (0.5, 6) not make sense as a solution for $y = 2x + 5$?

Solve the problems.

1   Mr. Wise is ordering a set of books for his class. Each book costs $6. There is a flat shipping fee
of $5. The table below shows the relationship between the total cost, c, and the number of
books, b. Fill in the blanks to complete the table.

Number of Books, b	2		6		10
Total Cost ($), c	17	29		53	65

2   Based on the information in problem 1, choose True or False for each statement.

A   The total cost for 11 books is $77.   ☐ True   ☐ False

B   The total cost for 7 books is $47.   ☐ True   ☐ False

C   If Mr. Wise spent $137 on books, he bought 22 books.   ☐ True   ☐ False

D   If Mr. Wise buys only 1 book, he pays only $6.   ☐ True   ☐ False

E   To find the cost of 20 books, multiply 65 by 2.   ☐ True   ☐ False

3   On a road map, 1 inch represents 2.25 miles. Which statement or graph correctly represents
this relationship? Circle all that apply.

A $m = 2.25i$, where i stands for the number of inches, and m stands for the number
of miles.

B   The ratio of inches to miles is 4 to 9.

C $i = 2.25m$, where m stands for the number of miles, and i stands for the number
of inches.

D   The ratio of inches to miles is 9 to 4.

E
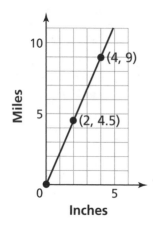

F
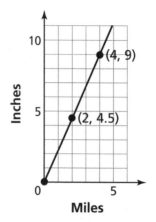

4   With a family bowling pass, families can bowl for $4 per game. The pass costs $10 per year. Use an equation, a table, and a graph to explain the relationship between the total amount of money spent on bowling in a year, *a*, and the number of games a family plays in a year, *g*.

Part A

Use words and an equation to represent this problem.

Part B

Create a table to show values for *g* and *a*.

Part C

Use the values from your table to draw a graph.

 **Self Check**   *Go back and see what you can check off on the Self Check on page 143.*

Solve the problems.

1 Which of the following is equivalent to the expression $\frac{1}{4} \times \frac{1}{4} \times \frac{1}{4} \times \frac{1}{4}$?

A $4 \times \frac{1}{4}$

B $\left(\frac{1}{4}\right)^4$

C $\left(\frac{1}{4}\right)^{16}$

D $4^{\frac{1}{4}}$

2 Which question can be answered by using the equation $5x = 150$?

A Leslie must divide 150 pieces of candy equally among 5 bags. How many pieces, x, will each bag hold?

B Mario will split 30 marigold plants among 5 garden plots. How many plants, x, will each plot hold?

C Nel wants to run 30 miles over the next 5 days. How many miles, x, will she run during that time?

D Omar plans to sell 150 calendars for a fundraiser in the next 30 days. How many calendars, x, must he sell each day to reach his goal?

3 Which student wrote an expression equivalent to $6x + 4x^3$? Circle all that apply.

A Anne wrote $(6 + x) + (4 + x^3)$.

B Bart wrote $6x(1 + \frac{2}{3}x^2)$.

C Cassie wrote $3x + 3x + 2x^3 + 2x^3$.

D David wrote $x(6 + 4x^2)$.

E Edgar wrote $10 + x^4$.

4 The table shows the total cost for different numbers of nights at a campground. Choose True or False for each statement.

Number of nights, n	2	5	7	12
Total cost, c	$32	$80	$112	$192

A The independent variable is c, and the dependent variable is n.

☐ True   ☐ False

B It would cost $96 to stay at the campground 6 nights.

☐ True   ☐ False

C If Danielle spent $48 for a campsite, then she paid for 3 nights.

☐ True   ☐ False

D The equation $c = 16n$ can be used to represent this situation.

☐ True   ☐ False

5   What is the value of $\dfrac{3x^2 - 3(y - 8)}{x + 2y}$ when $x = -4$ and $y = 4$?

Show your work.

Answer _____

6   Kimberly is selling popcorn for a fundraiser at school. Each student needs to sell a minimum of 20 buckets of popcorn. Kimberly has sold 8 buckets so far.

Part A

Write an inequality to represent the number of buckets, b, Kimberly still needs to sell.

Show your work.

Answer _____

Part B

In the space below, draw a number line. Then graph the inequality on that number line. Give your graph a title.

Performance Task

Answer the questions and show all your work on separate paper.

Shawn makes bracelets using stone beads. He buys the beads for $0.30 each. The wire used to make each bracelet costs $0.10.

A. Write an expression to find the cost to make a bracelet with *b* beads.

B. One of Shawn's popular bracelets, the Charmer, includes 15 stone beads. Another bracelet, the Sparkler, uses 20 beads. How much does it cost to make each bracelet?

C. The Charmer bracelet sells for $8 and the Sparkler sells for $12. Write equations and make graphs to show the relationship between the number of each kind of bracelet Shawn sells and the money he makes.

D. Shawn has 2,400 beads to make bracelets for an upcoming craft fair. He can use all the beads to make the Charmer bracelet, all the beads to make the Sparkler bracelet, or he can make a combination of both. Consider the cost of making each kind of bracelet and the amount he makes from selling them. What kind and how many bracelets do you suggest that Shawn make for the craft fair? Justify your answer.

✓ CHECKLIST
Did you . . .
☐ Write and evaluate expressions?
☐ Use an equation to make a graph?
☐ Consider different options before making your suggestion?

Reflect on Mathematical Practices

After you complete the task, choose one of the following questions to answer.

1. **Model** What are the different models you used to represent the relationships in this problem?

2. **Reason Mathematically** What kind of reasoning did you use when you developed your suggestion for Shawn?

A box seems like a pretty simple object. But a box can be so useful. You can fill a gift box with pretty stones for a present. But what volume of stones will the box hold? You can wrap a box with paper for a present. How much paper will you need? A box can be flattened out so you can save it in your desk drawer to use another day. What will it look like when it is flat?

In this unit you will draw polygons, join polygons together to make other polygons and three-dimensional figures. You will also use formulas to find the volume of three-dimensional figures and the area of their faces.

✓ Self Check

Before starting this unit, check off the skills you know below. As you complete each lesson, see how many more you can check off!

I can:	Before this unit	After this unit
find the area of triangles, quadrilaterals, and other polygons	☐	☐
solve problems with polygons in the coordinate plane	☐	☐
use nets to find the surface area of three-dimensional figures	☐	☐
find the volume of a rectangular prism with fractional edge lengths, for example: the volume of a cube with edges $\frac{1}{2}$ inch is $\frac{1}{8}$ cubic inch	☐	☐

Lesson 22   Part 1: Introduction

Area of Polygons

CCSS
6.G.A.1

You know how to find the area of a rectangle. Take a look at this problem.

The design of this stained glass window includes many different shapes. How much glass is needed to cover one of the parallelograms if its height measures 3 inches and its base measures 8 inches?

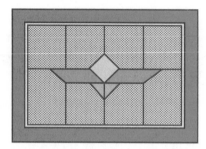

🔍 Explore It

Use the math you already know to solve this problem.

- You can draw the parallelogram on grid paper. Imagine cutting the parallelogram along the dotted line and moving the triangle you just cut off to the other side as shown below.

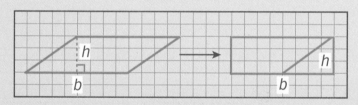

- What kind of shape do you get? _____

- How do you find the area of the new shape? _____

- If the base is 8 inches and the height is 3 inches, what is the area of the rectangle?

  _____

- Is the area of the parallelogram the same as the area of the rectangle? Explain your reasoning.

  _____

- How could you find the area of the parallelogram? _____

Find Out More

You saw that the formula for the area of a parallelogram is $A = bh$.

You can figure out how to find the area of a triangle in much the same way. Start with a rectangle. Then, draw a diagonal to split the rectangle in half.

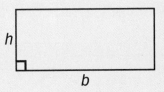

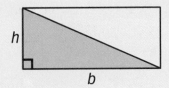

The sides of a rectangle are perpendicular to each other, so the triangles you get are right triangles. The area of one of the right triangles is $\frac{1}{2}$ the area of the rectangle.

What about other types of triangles? Start with a parallelogram. Drawing a diagonal splits the parallelogram in half.

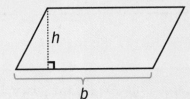

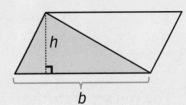

The area of the parallelogram is $A = bh$. The area of the triangle is $\frac{1}{2}$ the area of the parallelogram.

The base is always one of the sides of a triangle. It doesn't have to be the side the triangle is sitting on. The height to the base is always a perpendicular segment drawn to the base. Sometimes the height is drawn outside the triangle.

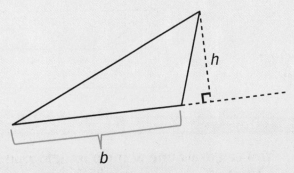

You can always put two triangles together to make a parallelogram.

Area of a triangle $= \frac{1}{2}bh$

Reflect

1 Describe the relationship between the area of a parallelogram and the area of a triangle that have the same base and height.

_____

_____

Read the problem below. Then explore how to find the area of a figure by breaking it up into triangles and parallelograms.

A part of another stained glass window design is shown below. How much glass would you need for this part of the window?

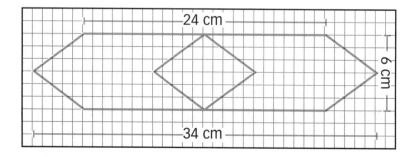

Picture It

You can separate the figure into two triangles and four parallelograms.

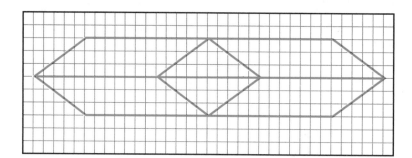

Model It

You can draw one of the parallelograms and one of the triangles and label them with their dimensions.

Solve It

You can use formulas to find the areas of the triangles and the parallelograms to solve the problem.

Area of a triangle $= \frac{1}{2}bh$

Area of a parallelogram $= bh$

Connect It

Now you use your drawings and formulas for the area of a triangle and a parallelogram to solve the problem on the previous page.

2 Look at Picture It. Explain how you could find the total area of the figure.

_____

_____

3 What can you say about the four parallelograms? The two triangles?

_____

_____

4 What is the area of one of the parallelograms? What is the area of one of the triangles? Show your work.

_____

5 Calculate the amount of glass needed for the window. Show your work.

_____

_____

6 Explain how you can find the area of a polygon.

_____

_____

_____

Try It

Use what you learned about finding the area of polygons to find the areas of the figures below. Show your work on a separate sheet of paper.

7
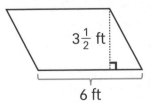
$3\frac{1}{2}$ ft

6 ft

8
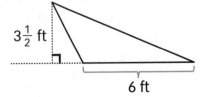
$3\frac{1}{2}$ ft

6 ft

Read the problem below. Then explore one way to find the area of a trapezoid.

In art class, Swati created a trapezoid made up of smaller trapezoids that are all the same size and shape. If the height of the large trapezoid is 4 inches and the bases measure 5 inches and 10 inches, what is the area of the large trapezoid? What is the area of one of the small trapezoids?

🔍 Picture It

You can draw the large trapezoid and label it with the information you know.

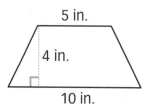

🔍 Model It

You can separate the trapezoid into two triangles and one rectangle and label their dimensions.

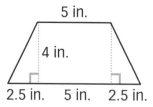

🔍 Solve It

You can find the areas of the triangles and the rectangle to help you solve the problem.

Area of a triangle $= \frac{1}{2} bh$

Area of a rectangle $= bh$

💡 Connect It

Now you will solve the problem by finding the areas of the triangles and the rectangle.

9 Look at Model It. What can you say about the two triangles that make up the trapezoid?

_____

10 How do you know that one of the sides of the right triangles is 2.5 inches?

_____

_____

11 Explain how to calculate the area of the large trapezoid. Show your work.

_____

_____

_____

12 What is the area of one of the small trapezoids? Show your work and explain your reasoning.

_____

_____

✏️ Try It

Use what you just learned about finding the area of a trapezoid to find the areas of the trapezoids below. Show your work on a separate sheet of paper.

13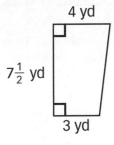
4 yd
$7\frac{1}{2}$ yd
3 yd

14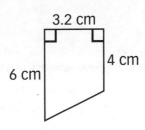
3.2 cm
4 cm
6 cm

Study the student model below. Then solve problems 15–17.

The student drew a large rectangle around the polygon and subtracted the areas of the four small squares from the area of the large rectangle.

Student Model

Find the area of this polygon.

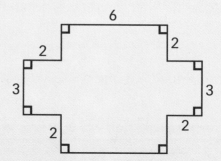

Look at how you could show your work.

The large rectangle is 10 by 7. The area is 10(7) = 70.

The area of a small square at a corner is 2(2) = 4. There is a square at each corner so the total area of the squares is 16.

The area of the polygon is 70 − 16 or 54.

Solution: ___54 square units___

Pair/Share

Could you solve this problem another way?

How can you separate the trapezoid into other shapes?

15 Mr. Millar's garden is in the shape of a trapezoid shown below. What is the area of his garden?

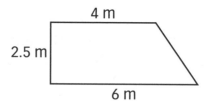

Show your work.

Pair/Share

How could you check to see if your answer makes sense?

Solution: _____

16 A triangular flag has the same area as a rectangle that is 6 ft by 7 ft. If the length of the base of the flag is 6 ft, what is the height of the flag?

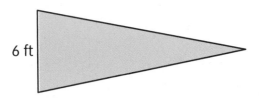

6 ft

Show your work.

What do you need to find first to solve this problem?

Solution: _____

◆Pair/Share

How is this problem different from ones you have seen before in this lesson?

17 If you double the lengths of each side of a rectangle, what can you say about the area of the new rectangle?

A The area of the new rectangle is half the original area.

B The area of the new rectangle is double the original area.

C The area of the new rectangle is four times the original area.

D The area of the new rectangle is eight times the original area.

Manuel chose **B** as the correct answer. How did he get that answer?

_____

_____

Would drawing a diagram and trying different cases help?

◆Pair/Share

How could you help Manuel answer the question?

Solve the problems.

1 Which triangle below has the greatest area?

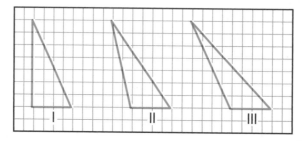

   A   Triangle I

   B   Triangle II

   C   Triangle III

   D   They all have the same area.

2 The trapezoid below is made up of a square and a triangle. The total area of the trapezoid is 57.5 square meters. The area of the triangle is 32.5 square meters. What is the length of a side of the square?

   A   5 meters

   B   25 meters

   C   90 meters

   D   Not enough information is given.

3 The diagram below shows an 18-foot by 40-foot pool surrounded by a 4-foot wide walkway. What is the area of the walkway?

[   ] square feet

4   Max needs to paint a wall surrounding a door. The dimensions on his blueprint are shown below.

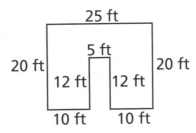

Which expression can he use to find the area of the wall? Select all that apply.

A $(20 \times 25) - (5 \times 12)$

B $10 \times 12 + 10 \times 12 + 8 \times 25$

C $10 \times 20 + 10 \times 20 + 5 \times 8$

D $(20 \times 15) + (20 \times 10)$

5   Triangle *RST* is drawn inside rectangle *RSNM*. Point *T* is halfway between points *M* and *N* on the rectangle. The length of side *RS* is 9 in. and the length of side *RM* is 8 in.

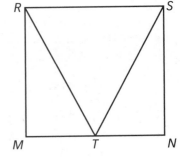

Show your work.

Part A   What is the area of triangle *RST*? _____

Part B   What is the ratio of the area of triangle *RST* to the area of triangle *RMT*?

_____

_____

_____

Part C   What is the ratio of the area of rectangle *RSNM* to the area of triangle *TSN*?

_____

_____

_____

✓ **Self Check**   *Go back and see what you can check off on the Self Check on page 219.*

Lesson 23   Part 1: Introduction 👥

Polygons in the Coordinate Plane

CCSS
6.G.A.3

You've learned about plane figures such as rectangles and triangles. In this lesson you will learn how to use coordinates to analyze plane figures. Take a look at this problem.

Cheryl walks her dogs after school. The routes she takes are shown on the coordinate grid to the right. Route 1 starts at point *A* and continues to points *B*, *C*, *D*, and back to *A*. Route 2 starts at *P* and goes to *Q*, *R*, *S*, and back to *P*. Which route is longer?

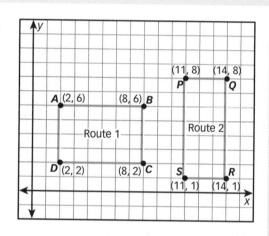

🔍 Explore It

Use the math you already know to solve this problem.

▪ Which pairs of points on Route 1 have the same *x*-coordinates? _____

_____

The same *y*-coordinates? _____

_____

▪ The way to find the distance between two points that have the same *x*-coordinate or the same *y*-coordinate is by counting the units between them. Look at Route 1. Find the distance from *A* to *B*, _____ from *B* to *C*, _____ from *C* to *D*, _____ and from *D* to *A* _____. The total distance is _____.

▪ Look at Route 2. Find the distance from *P* to *Q*, _____ from *Q* to *R*, _____ from *R* to *S*, _____ and from *S* to *P* _____. The total distance is _____.

▪ Explain how you can find which of the two routes is longer.

_____

_____

Find Out More

Each of Cheryl's routes on the previous page forms a rectangle on a coordinate plane. A rectangle is one type of polygon. A **polygon** is a closed plane figure whose sides are line segments that intersect only at their endpoints.

On the coordinate plane, if a side of a polygon is on a horizontal line, then its endpoints have the same *y*-coordinate. If a side of a polygon is on a vertical line, its endpoints have the same *x*-coordinate.

One way to find the length of a horizontal or vertical segment is by counting. The length of a segment is always a positive number.

It is often helpful to place a vertex or a side of the polygon on one of the axes of the coordinate plane, as shown in the diagrams below.

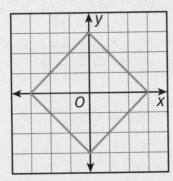
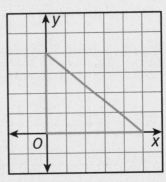

Reflect

1 Explain how you could find the distance between points (3, 6) and (7, 6) on the coordinate plane.

_____

_____

_____

_____

_____

Read the problem below. Then use what you know about rectangles and coordinates to find missing coordinates and dimensions.

An athletic director is planning to refinish the floor of a rectangular athletic court. Three corners of the court have the coordinates (−4, 2), (−4, −3), and (8, 2). Find the coordinates of the fourth corner and the perimeter of the court.

🔍 Graph It

You can graph the information that is given and then sketch the rectangle.

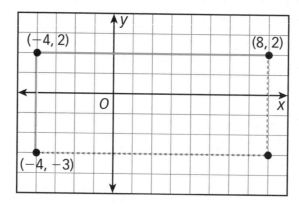

Draw a horizontal line that goes through (−4, −3) and a vertical line that goes through (8, 2). The point where they intersect is the fourth corner of the court.

To find the perimeter of the court, find its length and width. The length is the distance from (−4, 2) to (8, 2). The width is the distance from (−4, 2) to (−4, −3).

🔍 Model It

You can use words to describe the location of the fourth corner of the athletic court.

The fourth corner of the rectangle is on a vertical line that goes through (8, 2), so its *x*-coordinate is 8.

The fourth corner of the rectangle is on a horizontal line that goes through (−4, −3), so its *y*-coordinate is −3.

Connect It

Now you will solve the problems from the previous page using your understanding of coordinates and polygons.

2 What are the coordinates of the fourth corner of the rectangle? Explain how you found it.

_____

_____

3 Explain how to find the distance between $(-4, 2)$ and $(8, 2)$ using absolute value.

_____

_____

4 Explain how to count to find the distance between $(-4, 2)$ and $(-4, -3)$.

_____

_____

5 Describe how to find the perimeter of the athletic court.

_____

_____

_____

6 Explain why it is useful to know how to find distances on the coordinate plane both by counting and by using absolute value.

_____

_____

Try It

Use what you just learned about polygons on a coordinate plane to solve these problems. Show your work on a separate sheet of grid paper.

7 The coordinates of three corners of a square are $(-2, 0)$, $(1, 0)$, and $(1, -3)$. Graph these three points. What are the coordinates of the fourth corner of the square? _____ Draw the square.

8 What is the perimeter of the square in problem 7? _____

Read the problem below. Then explore how to find the area of a polygon on a coordinate plane.

On a map of a county park, the park entrance is located at (0, 0), a community garden is located at (4, 3), and a playground is located at (8, 0).

• What shape is formed by a path connecting the three locations?

• The park's director is planning to grow grass inside the shape formed by the path. What is the area of the shape?

 **Graph It**

You can make a graph showing the given information to help solve the problem.

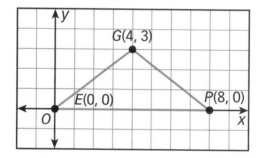

The park entrance is labeled *E*, the community garden is labeled *G*, and the playground is labeled *P*.

The polygon is a triangle with a base of 8 units and a height of 3 units.

Solve It

You can use the formula for the area of a triangle to solve the problem.

Area $= \left(\frac{1}{2}\right) \times$ base $\times$ height

$A = \left(\frac{1}{2}\right)bh$

$= \left(\frac{1}{2}\right)(8)(3)$

$= \left(\frac{1}{2}\right)24$

$= 12$

The area of the triangle is 12 square units.

Connect It

Now you will explain how to solve the problem from the previous page using your understanding of polygons on a coordinate plane.

9 Explain how you know that the base of the triangle is 8 units long.

_____

_____

10 Explain how you know that the height of the triangle is 3 units long.

_____

11 Kristina divided △EGP into two smaller triangles by drawing a vertical line from G to the x-axis, as shown in the diagram.

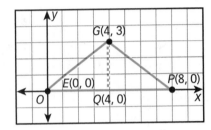

What do you notice about △EGQ and △PGQ?

_____

12 How could you use Kristina's method to find the area of △EGP?

_____

_____

13 Suppose that the coordinates of point G were (4, −3) instead of (4, 3). Would the area of △EGP be the same? Explain why or why not.

_____

_____

Try It

Use what you just learned about finding the area of a polygon on the coordinate plane to solve these problems. Show your work on a separate sheet of paper.

A baseball diamond is in the shape of a square, with bases at (0, 4), (4, 0), (0, −4), and (−4, 0). The pitcher's mound is located at (0, 0).

14 What is the area of the part of the square that is in Quadrant I? _____

15 What is the total area of the square? _____

Study the student model below. Then solve problems 16–18.

The student divided the polygon into two rectangles and found the area of each one.

Student Model

Find the area of the polygon shown below.

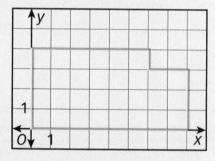

Look at how you can divide the polygon into shapes whose areas are easy to find.

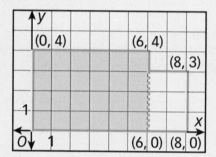

Area of shaded rectangle: (6)(4) = 24

Area of unshaded rectangle: (2)(3) = 6

Solution: The total area is 24 + 6 = 30 square units.

💬 **Pair/Share**

Is there another way to divide the shape into two rectangles?

How can you separate this figure into different shapes?

16 Find the area of the trapezoid.

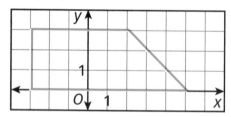

Show your work.

💬 **Pair/Share**

Explain the steps you used to find the area.

Solution: _____

17 Find the area of the parallelogram.

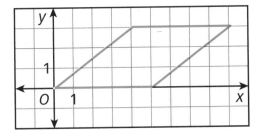

Show your work.

Solution: _____

18 A swimming pool and the deck surrounding it are shown in the coordinate plane below. What is the area of the deck? Circle the letter of the correct answer.

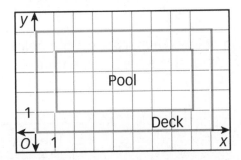

A 66 square units

B 21 square units

C 24 square units

D 45 square units

Ron chose **D** as his answer. Why is this answer incorrect?

_____

_____

_____

Solve the problems.

1 Three corners of a rectangular city block are located at (2, 2), (2, −4), and (−5, −4) on a coordinate plane. What are the coordinates of the fourth corner?

A (−5, 8)

B (5, −2)

C (−5, 2)

D (2, −5)

2 What is the perimeter of the rectangular city block in problem 1?

A 13 units

B 26 units

C 42 units

D 10 units

3 On the coordinate plane, plot the following points. Then, connect the points in order from *A* to *E* and then back to *A* to form a figure. What is the area of the figure?

A(1, 2)   *B*(1, 7)   *C*(9, 7)   *D*(9, 3)   *E*(6, 5)

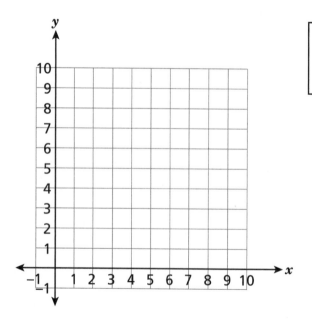

The area of the figure is

☐ square units.

4 Which triangle has an area of 22.5 square units? Circle all that apply.

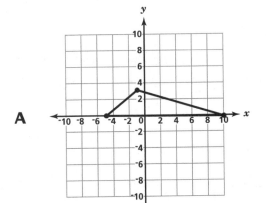

A

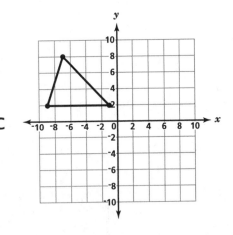

C

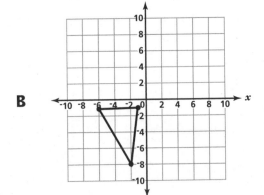

B

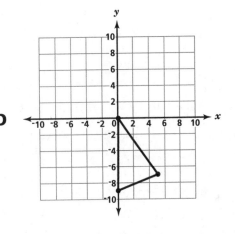

D

5 The rectangle on the coordinate plane below is a diagram of a flag. Each of the large triangles on the flag will be a different color. Is the same amount of material needed for each color? Explain why or why not.

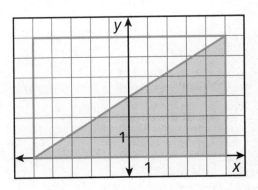

_____

_____

6 Two vertices of a triangle are (0, 0) and (8, 0). The x-coordinate of the third vertex is 4. Imagine that you draw, on a coordinate plane, several triangles that meet all these conditions. What would be the same about all the triangles you drew? What would be different?

_____

 **Self Check** *Go back and see what you can check off on the Self Check on page 219.*

Lesson 24   Part 1: Introduction 👥

Nets and Surface Area

CCSS
6.G.A.4

You know how to find the areas of rectangles and triangles. In this lesson you will learn how to find the surface area of three-dimensional figures such as prisms and pyramids. Take a look at this problem.

How can you find the sum of the areas of the faces of this box?

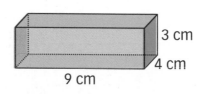

3 cm
4 cm
9 cm

🔍 Explore It

Use the math you already know to solve this problem.

Imagine cutting the box open along its edges and laying it flat.

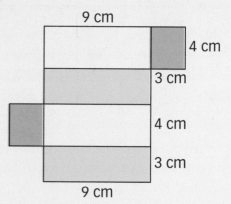

9 cm
4 cm
3 cm
4 cm
3 cm
9 cm

- How many faces does the box have? _____ What shapes are they? _____ How many different sizes of rectangles are there? _____

- How do you find the area of a rectangle?
  _____

- What are the dimensions of the different faces?

  Front and back: _____ cm by _____ cm

  Top and bottom: _____ cm by _____ cm

  Left and right sides: _____ cm by _____ cm

- Find the area of each rectangle. Write the number of square centimeters of area inside each one shown in the diagram above.

- Suppose you needed to paint the box. Explain how you could find the area you need to cover.

  _____

  _____

Find Out More

In the problem on the previous page, a rectangular prism is cut and "unfolded" into a flat representation called a **net**. Each face of the prism is shown in the net.

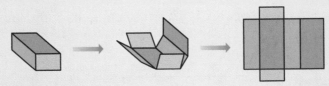

You can use a net to find surface area of any three-dimensional figure. The **surface area** is the sum of the areas of the faces of the figure.

You can draw nets for other three-dimensional figures. The **triangular prism** below has two parallel triangular faces that are the same size and shape, called **bases**, and three rectangular faces. The rectangular faces can be different sizes.

A **pyramid** is a three-dimensional figure whose base is a polygon and whose other faces are triangles. The square pyramid shown below has a square base and four triangular faces that are the same size and shape.

Reflect

1 Explain in your own words how to use a net to find the surface area of a three-dimensional figure.

_____

_____

_____

Read the problem below. Then use what you know about the area of polygons to find the surface area of a rectangular prism.

A packaging designer wants to find out how much leather is needed to cover the jewelry box shown below. The box is 12 cm long, 3 cm wide, and 5 cm high. Find the surface area of the box.

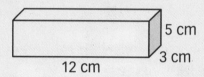

12 cm · 5 cm · 3 cm

🔍 Picture It

You can draw and use a net of the box to help you find the surface area.

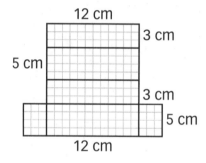

12 cm · 3 cm · 5 cm · 3 cm · 5 cm · 12 cm

🔍 Model It

You can use a table to organize the information you need.

Face	Length (cm)	Width (cm)	Height (cm)	Area (sq cm)
Top	12	3	–	36
Bottom	12	3	–	36
Front	12	–	5	60
Back	12	–	5	60
Right side	–	3	5	15
Left side	–	3	5	15

Connect It

Now you will use what you know about the area of rectangles and your understanding of surface area to solve the problem on the previous page.

2 Look at the table in Model It. How could you find the total surface area of the rectangular prism? _____

What is the surface area of the prism? Show your work. _____

_____

3 In a rectangular prism, which pairs of faces have the same areas?

_____

4 How can you use your answer to problem 3 to find the surface area of a prism?

_____

_____

5 Use the method from problem 4 to find the surface area. Show your work.

_____

_____

6 Explain how to find the surface area of a rectangular prism.

_____

_____

Try It

Use what you learned about finding the surface area of a prism to find the surface area of the rectangular prisms below.

7

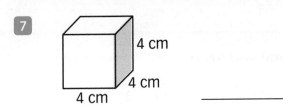

4 cm

4 cm

4 cm

_____

8

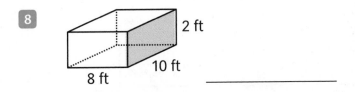

2 ft

10 ft

8 ft

_____

Read the problem below. Then explore how to find the surface area of a triangular prism.

The triangular prism shown below has a triangular base with length 12 cm and height 8 cm. The height of the prism is 11 cm. What is the surface area of the prism?

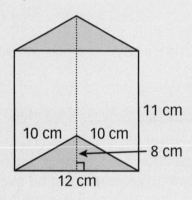

🔍 Picture It

You can draw and label a net of the prism to find its surface area.

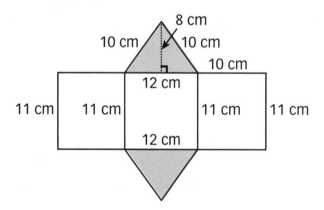

🔍 Model It

You can use a table to organize the information you need.

Face	Base (cm)	Height (cm)	Area (sq cm)
Triangle	12	8	48
Triangle	12	8	48
Rectangle	10	11	110
Rectangle	10	11	110
Rectangle	12	11	132

🔍 Connect It

Now you will use what you know about the area of triangles and rectangles and an understanding of surface area to solve the problem on the previous page.

9 How many faces of the prism on the previous page are triangles? Explain how to find the area of each triangle.

_____

10 How many faces of the prism are rectangles? Are they all the same shape and size?

_____

11 What is the surface area of the triangular prism? Show your work.

_____

_____

12 Explain how to find the surface area of any triangular prism.

_____

_____

✏️ Try It

Use what you learned about finding the surface area of a triangular prism to solve these problems. Show your work on a separate sheet of paper.

13 The mailing tube shown below is 36 inches long, 6 inches wide, and 5.2 inches deep. The bases are equilateral triangles. How much cardboard is used to make the tube?

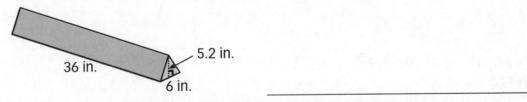

36 in.   5.2 in.   6 in.

_____

14 A display case is shaped like the prism shown below. The bases are right triangles. Find the surface area of the prism.

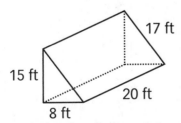

17 ft   15 ft   20 ft   8 ft

_____

Read the problem below. Then explore how to find the surface area of a pyramid.

Rebekah is planning to make a model of a pyramid for a geography project. The length of each edge of the base is 6 in., and the height of each triangular face is 5 in. How much cardboard will Rebekah need to make the pyramid?

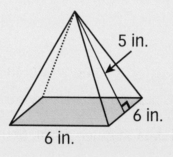

5 in.

6 in.

6 in.

 **Picture It**

You can label a net of the pyramid to find its total area.

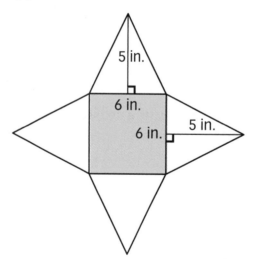

5 in.

6 in.

6 in.   5 in.

 **Model It**

You can use a table to organize the information you need.

Face	Base (in.)	Height (in.)	Area (sq in.)
Triangle	6	5	15
Triangle	6	5	15
Triangle	6	5	15
Triangle	6	5	15
Square	6	6	36

Connect It

Now you will use what you know about the area of triangles and rectangles and surface area to solve the problem on the previous page.

15 How many faces does the pyramid have? Describe them.

_____

16 How do you find the area of the base of the pyramid? _____

17 How do you find the total area of the triangular faces of the pyramid?

_____

_____

_____

18 What is the surface area of the pyramid? Show your work.

_____

_____

19 Explain how to find the surface area of a rectangular pyramid.

_____

Try It

Use what you learned about finding the surface area of a pyramid to solve these problems. Show your work on a separate sheet of paper.

20 Rebekah decides to make her pyramid model much larger, so the length of each edge of the base is 60 in. and the height of each triangular face is 50 in. What is the surface area of this larger pyramid? _____

21 Find the surface area of the pyramid shown below. The base is a rectangle and the opposite triangle faces are the same size and shape.

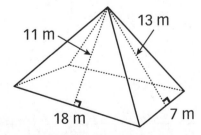

_____

Study the student model below. Then solve problems 22–24.

The student wrote the area of each face on the net of the prism.

A gift box is 16 in. long, $9\frac{1}{2}$ in. wide, and 4 in. high. How much wrapping paper is needed to cover the box?

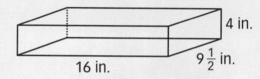

4 in.

$9\frac{1}{2}$ in.

16 in.

You can use a diagram to organize the information.

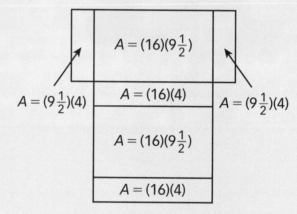

$A = (16)(9\frac{1}{2})$

$A = (9\frac{1}{2})(4)$ $A = (16)(4)$ $A = (9\frac{1}{2})(4)$

$A = (16)(9\frac{1}{2})$

$A = (16)(4)$

Solution: $\underline{2(152) + 2(38) + 2(64) = 508; \text{ 508 sq in. of paper}}$

Pair/Share

Can you find the surface area without using a net?

How many faces are rectangles and how many are triangles?

22 What is the surface area of this triangular prism? The base of each triangle is 42 m and the height of the triangular base is 20 m.

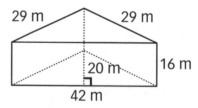

29 m   29 m

20 m   16 m

42 m

Show your work.

Pair/Share

Did you find the area of each face of the prism separately, or did you use some shortcuts?

Solution: _____

23 Does the net shown below fold up into a prism or a pyramid? Find the surface area of the figure formed by the net.

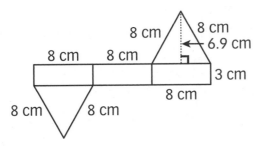

Can a pyramid have just two triangular faces?

Show your work.

Solution: _____

_____

_____

_____

Pair/Share

How can you use the net to find the area of all the rectangular faces?

24 An open storage box is shaped like a square prism but without a top face. The base of the box is a square with side length 12 in., and the height of the box is 10 in. What is the surface area of the box?

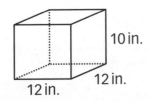

How is this problem different from the others?

A   600 square inches

B   624 cubic inches

C   768 square inches

D   1,440 square inches

Braden chose **C** as the correct answer. Why is his answer incorrect?

_____

_____

_____

Pair/Share

Explain what the correct answer should be.

Solve the problems.

1   A rectangular prism has a base that is 1.5 meters by 2 meters, and the prism is 4 meters high. What is the surface area of the prism?

A   28 m²   **C**   12 m²

B   34 m²   **D**   31 m²

2   Which diagram represents the net of a cube? Circle all that apply.

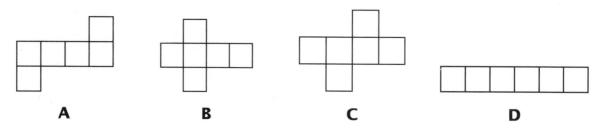

   A   **B**   **C**   **D**

3   Decide whether or not each expression correctly calculates the surface area of the triangular prism represented by the net below. Select Yes or No for each expression.

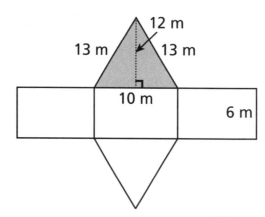

A $(12 \times 10) + (12 \times 13) + (10 \times 6)$ ☐ Yes   ☐ No

B $(2 \times 13) + (2 \times 13) + 2 \times (6 + 13) + 60$ ☐ Yes   ☐ No

C $\frac{1}{2}(10 \times 12) + \frac{1}{2}(10 \times 12) + 2(6 \times 13) + 60$ ☐ Yes   ☐ No

D $2(13 + 13 + 12 + 6 + 10) + 60$ ☐ Yes   ☐ No

E $\frac{1}{2}(13 \times 12) + \frac{1}{2}(13 \times 12) + 2(6 \times 10 \times 13)$ ☐ Yes   ☐ No

4   Two rectangular prisms each have a surface area of 600 square inches. What are the possible dimensions of the prisms?

Show your work.

Prism 1 _____

Prism 2 _____

5   In the space below, sketch a prism, using any dimensions that you like. Then sketch a larger prism whose dimensions are *twice* the dimensions of your first prism.

Part A

Find the surface area of each prism.

Show your work.

Prism 1 _____   *Prism 2* _____

Part B

What is the ratio of the surface area of the smaller prism to the surface area of the larger prism?

Show your work.

Answer _____

✓ **Self Check**   *Go back and see what you can check off on the Self Check on page 219.*

Lesson 25   Part 1: Introduction 👥

Volume

You know how to find the volume of a prism whose dimensions are whole numbers. In this lesson, you will find the volume when the dimensions include fractions. Take a look at this problem.

Each edge of a cube is 1 yard long. The cube is going to be filled with small cubes. Each small cube has edges that are 1 foot long. (Remember that there are 3 feet in 1 yard.)

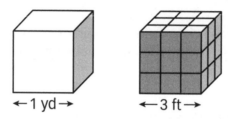

←1 yd→   ←3 ft→

What is the volume, in cubic yards, of one of the small cubes?

🔍 Explore It

Use the math you already know to solve this problem.

- Write the volume of the large cube in cubic yards. _____

- How many small cubes are there along one edge of the large cube? _____

- How many small cubes form one layer of the large cube? _____

- How many layers are there? _____

- How many small cubes are needed to fill the large cube? _____

- Explain how to find the volume of one of the small cubes in cubic yards. What is the volume, in cubic yards, of each small cube?

  _____

  _____

  _____

🔍 Find Out More

Prisms in everyday life may have dimensions that are fractional. The length (l), width (w), and height (h) of the small cubes on the previous page are all $\frac{1}{3}$ yard.

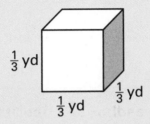

$\frac{1}{3}$ yd

$\frac{1}{3}$ yd

$\frac{1}{3}$ yd

You can use the formulas $V = lwh$ or $V = Bh$ to find the volume of any rectangular prism, whether the side lengths are whole numbers, fractions, or decimals.

$V = l \times w \times h$

$\quad = \frac{1}{3}$ yd $\cdot \frac{1}{3}$ yd $\cdot \frac{1}{3}$ yd

$\quad = \frac{1 \cdot 1 \cdot 1}{3 \cdot 3 \cdot 3}$ yd³

$\quad = \frac{1}{27}$ cubic yard, or yd³

✏️ Reflect

1 Explain how to find the volume of a cube whose edge length is $\frac{1}{4}$ yd. Then find the volume of such a cube.

_____

_____

_____

Read the problem below. Then explore different ways to find the volume of a rectangular prism whose dimensions are not all whole numbers.

A child's sandbox is 5 feet wide, 4 feet long, and 3 feet deep. Grace fills the sandbox so that the sand is $2\frac{1}{2}$ feet deep. What is the volume of the sand in the box?

🔍 Picture It

You can make a sketch of the sandbox and label it with the given information.

The sand is $2\frac{1}{2}$ feet deep, so $h = 2\frac{1}{2}$.

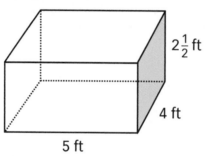

🔍 Model It

You can model the volume of the sand with 1-foot unit cubes.

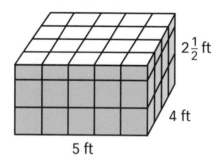

Connect It

Now you can use what you know about volume to find the volume of sand in the sandbox.

2 Look at Model It. How many cubes are in the bottom layer? Explain your reasoning.

_____

_____

How many cubes in the next layer? _____

3 How many whole cubes can you make with the blocks in the third layer? Explain.

_____

_____

4 Explain how to use your answers to problems 2 and 3 to find the total volume of sand.

_____

_____

5 Use the formula $V = lwh$ to find the total volume of the sand.

_____

6 Describe how to find the volume of a rectangular prism when the dimensions include fractions.

_____

_____

Try It

Use what you learned about finding the volume of a prism to solve these problems. Show your work on a separate sheet of paper.

7 The length of a box of colored pencils is 6 inches, the width is 4 inches, and the height is $\frac{3}{8}$ inch. What is the volume of the box? _____

8 The width of a recycling bin is $\frac{3}{4}$ foot, the length is 1 foot, and the height is $1\frac{1}{2}$ feet. What is the volume of the recycling bin? _____

Read the problem below. Then explore different ways to find one dimension of a rectangular prism whose dimensions are not all whole numbers.

The volume of water in an aquarium is 1,150 cubic inches. The base of the aquarium is a square with edge length 10 inches. What is the height of the water in the aquarium?

Picture It

You can make a sketch of the water in the aquarium and label it with the given information.

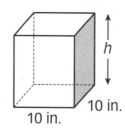

10 in.

10 in.

10 in.

h

Model It

You can model the volume of water with the equation $V = l \times w \times h$ or $V = B \times h$.

$V = l \times w \times h$

$1{,}150 = 10 \times 10 \times h$

In the formula $V = Bh$, B represents the area of the base of the prism. To find the area of the base, multiply 10 inches by 10 inches to get 100 square inches.

$V = B \times h$

$1{,}150 = 100 \times h$

💡 Connect It

Now you can use what you know about volume to find the height of the water in the aquarium.

9 Explain how the formulas $V = lwh$ and $V = Bh$ are alike.

_____

_____

10 Describe how to solve the equation $1,150 = 100 \times h$ for h.

_____

_____

11 Find the height of the water in the aquarium.

_____

12 Suppose you know that the height of the water in the aquarium is $11\frac{1}{2}$ inches, the length is 10 inches, and the volume is 1,150 cubic inches. Write the equation you might use to find the width of the aquarium.

_____

13 Look back at how you found the volume of the sand in the sandbox. Compare finding the volume with finding the height of the water on these pages. How are the two processes different?

_____

_____

_____

✏️ Try It

Use what you learned about finding a missing dimension of a rectangular prism to solve these problems. Show your work on a separate sheet of paper.

14 A product design team is working on a new drink box, which will hold 225 cubic centimeters of juice. The box is 12.5 centimeters high and 4.5 centimeters long. What is the width of the box? _____

15 Eduardo has 27 cubic feet of wood chips to use for a new path in a garden. The chips must be 6 inches deep, and the path is 3 feet wide. How long can the path be? (Remember that there are 12 inches in 1 foot.) _____

©Curriculum Associates, LLC   Copying is not permitted.

Study the student model below. Then solve problems 16–18.

The student multiplied the length, width, and height to find the volume of the box.

Student Model

A box of breakfast cereal is 20 centimeters long, 7.5 centimeters wide, and 30 centimeters high. What is the volume of the box?

Look at how you can use a drawing to display the given information.

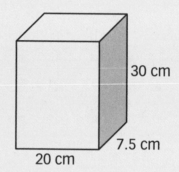

30 cm

7.5 cm

20 cm

$V = l \times w \times h$

$ = 20 \times 7.5 \times 30$

$ = 4,500$

Solution: **4,500 cubic centimeters**

💬 **Pair/Share**

How could you estimate the volume?

Sketching the prism is a good way to organize the given information.

16 The base of a jewelry box is a square with an edge length of $5\frac{1}{2}$ inches. The box is 2 inches high. What is the volume of the box?

Show your work.

💬 **Pair/Share**

If the base is a square, which two dimensions do you know?

Solution: _____

17 A rectangular swimming pool is 10 meters long and 4.5 meters wide. If the volume of the water in the pool is 72 cubic meters, how deep is the water?

Show your work.

What are you trying to find in this problem?

Solution: _____

18 The volume of a rectangular prism is 10 cubic feet. What could the dimensions of the prism be?

A   100 ft, $\frac{1}{2}$ ft, $\frac{1}{2}$ ft

B   10 ft, $\frac{1}{2}$ ft, 2 ft

C   5 ft, $2\frac{1}{2}$ ft, $2\frac{1}{2}$ ft

D   10 ft, 10 ft, $\frac{1}{2}$ ft

Carla chose **C** as the correct answer. How did she get that answer?

_____

_____

_____

_____

Will the formula for volume help answer the question?

Solve the problems.

1 What is the volume of a cube with edge length $\frac{2}{3}$ yard?

  A $\frac{4}{9}$ yd³

  B $\frac{8}{3}$ yd³

  C $\frac{8}{27}$ yd³

  D 2 yd³

2 The volume of a box of soup broth is 972 cubic centimeters. The box is 20 centimeters high and 10.8 centimeters long. How wide is the box?

  A 90 cm

  B 4.5 cm

  C 216 cm

  D 48.6 cm

3 The cargo hold of a truck is a rectangular prism measuring 18 feet by 13.5 feet by 9 feet. The driver needs to figure out how many storage boxes he can load. Choose True or False for each statement.

  A The truck driver can load up to 54 boxes with dimensions 3 ft by 3 ft by 4.5 ft. ☐ True ☐ False

  B The truck driver can load up to 81 boxes with dimensions 3 ft by 3 ft by 3 ft. ☐ True ☐ False

  C The truck driver can load up to 24 boxes with dimensions 4.5 ft by 4.5 ft by 4.5 ft. ☐ True ☐ False

  D The truck driver can load up to 12 boxes with dimensions 9 ft by 4.5 ft by 4.5 ft. ☐ True ☐ False

4 The three shipping boxes below have different volumes and are to be labeled Large, Medium, and Small based on their volumes. Write the appropriate label, Large, Medium, or Small, under each of the boxes.

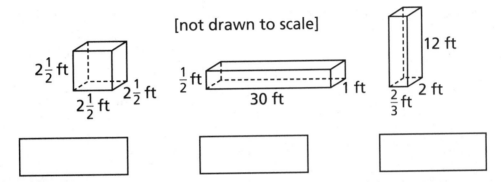

[not drawn to scale]

5 The volume of a rectangular prism is 12 cubic inches. One of the dimensions of the prism is a fraction. What could the dimensions of the prism be? Give two possible answers.

Show your work.

Answer _____

6 A building supply company sells sand by the cubic foot and by the cubic yard. The price of one cubic yard of sand is $33.75. What do you think the price of one cubic foot of sand should be? Explain your answer.

Show your work.

Answer _____

_____

_____

_____

✓ **Self Check** *Go back and see what you can check off on the Self Check on page 219.*

Solve the problems.

1 Sara is having linoleum installed in her laundry room. The laundry room floor is shown below.

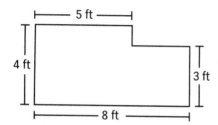

It costs $8 per square foot to install linoleum. What is the total cost to install linoleum in Sara's laundry room?

A $184

B $200

C $216

D $232

2 The trapezoid shown is divided into a right triangle and a rectangle.

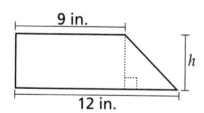

Can each expression be used to find the area of the trapezoid? Select Yes or No for expressions A–D.

A $9 \times h + 12 \times h$ ☐ Yes ☐ No

B $h(9 + 12)$ ☐ Yes ☐ No

C $\frac{h}{2}(9 + 12)$ ☐ Yes ☐ No

D $12h - \frac{3h}{2}$ ☐ Yes ☐ No

3 Gerald pours 441 cubic centimeters of liquid into the prism shown below. In the box, write the correct height of the liquid.

[not drawn to scale]

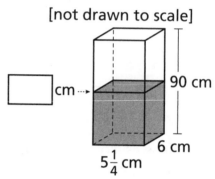

4 Maggie has a rectangular box with a length of $6\frac{1}{2}$ inches, a width 9 inches, and a height of $3\frac{1}{2}$ inches. What is the volume of Maggie's box?

Show your work.

Answer _____ cubic inches

5 Micah drew a rectangle on a coordinate grid. Three of the coordinates of the rectangle are (−4, 5), (−4, −3), and (6, 5).

Part A

Draw Micah's rectangle on the coordinate grid.

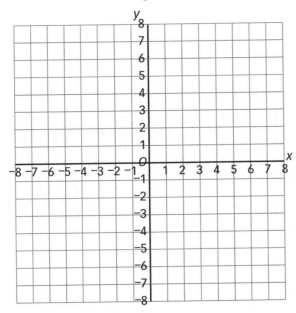

Part B

What is the perimeter of the rectangle?

Show your work.

Answer _____ units

Performance Task

Answer the questions and show all your work on separate paper.

A cereal company is designing a cardboard box for a new granola product. The box will hold 128 cubic inches of granola. The volume of the granola will be 80% of the volume of the box.

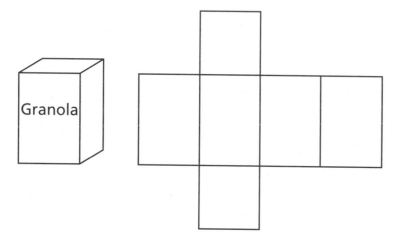

A. Find the volume of the box.

B. Create two possible designs for the box, each with different dimensions. Use grid paper to draw a net of each box. Then find the surface area of each box.

C. A supplier sells cardboard at a unit rate per square inch. Which of your boxes would cost less? Which design would you suggest that the cereal company use? Explain.

Reflect on Mathematical Practices

After you complete the task, choose one of the following questions to answer.

1. **Use Structure** How did you use multiplication to find the dimensions of the box?

2. **Model** How did drawing nets of the boxes help you find the surface area?

Restaurant owners need to collect information about the food they serve: What was the most popular dish on the restaurant's menu this week? City planners need to collect information about traffic patterns: How many cars travel east through this intersection each day? Coaches need to collect information about their players: How many points has each player scored during the season? Once you have collected some data, you need to know what to do with it to make it useful.

In this unit, you will learn how to organize data and use it to answer questions about the data.

✓ Self Check

Before starting this unit, check off the skills you know below. As you complete each lesson, see how many more you can check off!

I can:	Before this unit	After this unit
recognize what makes a question a statistical question	☐	☐
calculate measures of center such as mean and median	☐	☐
calculate measures of spread such as range and mean absolute deviation	☐	☐
display data accurately with a dot plot, histogram, or box plot	☐	☐
describe data using measures of center and measures of spread	☐	☐

Lesson 26 Part 1: Introduction 👥
Understand Statistical Questions

Why ask statistical questions?

When you want to find out more about something, one thing you can do is ask questions. Some questions have exact answers, such as, "How many people are in your class right now?" Other questions can have many answers, such as asking some sixth graders, "What is your favorite kind of music?"

When you want to find out what kind of music all sixth graders like most, there are likely too many people to ask. By asking 20 sixth graders, "What is your favorite kind of music?," you can get a good sense of the type of music all sixth graders like. If you asked another class of sixth graders the same question, your results would probably be similar but not exactly the same.

When you ask a question to make a prediction about a larger group, you are asking a statistical question. **Statistical questions** do not have an exact answer; you expect to get a variety of answers. So answers to statistical questions have variability. Non-statistical questions have exact answers.

🔍 **Think** What does it mean for a question to be statistical?

Sasha wants to collect statistical information about the different sports sixth graders at her school like to watch. She writes 3 questions to ask 50 sixth graders and will use the results to make a prediction about all sixth graders. Which questions are statistical and which are not?

> **Circle a statistical question where you might expect many different answers.**

- When is the next home basketball game?

- What is your favorite sport to watch?

- What was the last sports game you watched at this school?

The first question is not statistical because the date of the next home game is the same for no matter whom or how many people Sasha asks.

The next two questions are statistical because you would expect some variability in the answers. Sasha could use the responses to think about the different sports that sixth graders like to watch.

Think How do I write statistical questions?

What statistical question could Sasha ask if she was interested in knowing what school sport sixth graders like to watch the most?

Look at the questions Sasha wrote. "What is your favorite sport to watch?" is too general. Someone's favorite sport to watch might not be a school sport. There may be too many varying answers.

What are possible answers to this question? Are the answers too general? Too specific?

"What was the last sports game you watched at this school?" is too specific. Depending on the time of year or what home game was most recent, there may not be enough variability.

To collect data on what school sport sixth graders like to watch the most, Sasha could ask:

"Which school sport are you most interested in watching? Circle one from the list below."

Then Sasha could list all the school sports at her school.

Possible responses would be one of the listed sports. The varying answers would help Sasha draw conclusions about which sports sixth graders at her school most like to watch.

Now you'll have a chance to think more about statistical questions and the data they help collect.

Reflect

1 Explain the difference between a question that is statistical and one that is not.

_____

_____

_____

_____

Explore It

Determine whether each question is *statistical* or *non-statistical*. Then, explain your answer.

2 A political group asked voters waiting in line to vote: Who are the 2 major candidates running for president this year?

_____

_____

3 The journalism club surveyed students in the library and asked: About how much time do you spend reading each day?

_____

_____

4 To decide if a new movie should be shown this Friday, a movie theatre invited 50 people to view the movie and answer the question: Did you enjoy the movie?

_____

_____

5 A sixth grader asks her guidance counselor: How many clubs and sports are open to sixth graders at this school?

_____

_____

Write statistical questions.

6 Write both a statistical and a non-statistical question you could ask some classmates to make a prediction about teenagers and text messaging.

_____

_____

_____

Talk About It

Solve the problem below as a group.

7 Use an example from the previous page to explain what it means for a question to have statistical variability.

_____

_____

_____

8 Look at problems 2–5. How could you change one of the non-statistical questions so that it is statistical? Explain.

_____

_____

9 Look at the questions you wrote in problem 6. Explain why the answers do or don't have variability.

_____

_____

_____

Try It Another Way

Look at these survey results and think about a possible statistical question.

10 Mia surveyed her classmates to make a prediction about kids her age.

Hours	0	0.5	1	1.5	2
Number of Students	2	8	5	3	1

Which could be a question Mia asked? Explain.

- How many people do not watch TV?
- How many TV shows do you watch regularly?
- About how long do you spend watching TV everyday?

_____

_____

_____

Connect It

Talk through these problems as a class. Then write your answers below.

11 **Compare.** Which question is statistical and which is not? Explain how you know.

- What is your favorite Olympic sport to watch?
- When are the next Olympic games?

_____

_____

_____

_____

_____

12 **Analyze.** Which is a better statistical question to ask your classmates if you are interested in finding out movies sixth graders enjoy watching? Explain.

- What is the most recent movie you saw?
- What are three of your favorite movies?

_____

_____

_____

_____

_____

13 **Predict.** Which statistical question would result in more variability? Explain.

- Do you own a scooter and/or bicycle?
- About how many hours per week do sixth graders participate in sports?

_____

_____

_____

_____

Put It Together

Use what you have learned to complete this task.

14 Write statistical questions and analyze the variability in the answers.

A Write two statistical questions that you are interested in asking the students at your school.

_____

_____

B Choose one question to ask your classmates and record the answers in a line plot.

_____

C Explain how your classmates' answers showed variability.

_____

_____

_____

D Explain why you expect variability in the answers if you asked a different group of students the same question.

_____

_____

_____

_____

Lesson 27 Part 1: Introduction

Measures of Center and Variability

In the previous lesson, you learned that statistical data varies. In this lesson, you'll learn to explain variability in data. Take a look at this problem.

Students in band, chorus, and strings classes collected donations for a fundraiser concert to raise money for the music program. These line plots show the results of asking 10 students from each class how much money they collected.

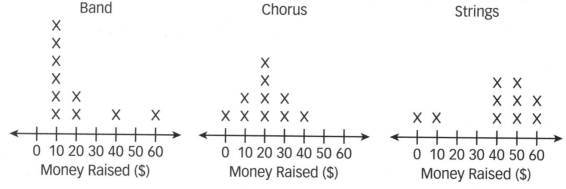

Use the shape of each line plot to explain how the data varies.

🔍 Explore It

Use the math you already know to solve this problem.

● Between what numbers are the most common responses for each group of students?

Band _____   Chorus _____   Strings _____

● Based on the shape of the line plot, which class likely raised the most money? Explain.

_____

_____

● Based on the shape of the line plot, which class likely raised the least money? Explain.

_____

● Do you think these graphs would look different if 10 more students were surveyed from each class? Explain.

_____

🔍 Find Out More

On the previous page, you looked at the shape of each line plot to think about what the data mean. You observed that the data for band were clustered around lesser values, and the data for strings were clustered around greater values. A **cluster** of data is a group of data points that crowd near each other.

Here are some other terms you can use to describe the shape of data points on a graph:

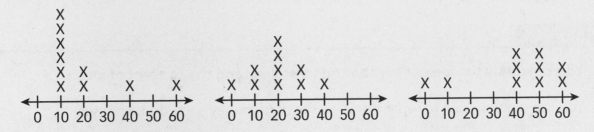

- ⬤ A graph is **skewed left** when most of the data points are clustered near higher values.

- ⬤ A graph is **skewed right** when most of the data points are clustered near lower values.

- ⬤ **Symmetrical** graphs show the same number of data points above and below a middle point.

- ⬤ A **peak** forms when many data points are at one value.

- ⬤ An **outlier** is a data point far away from the other data points; it doesn't quite fit with the rest of the data points.

✏️ Reflect

1 Can an outlier value be part of a cluster of values? Explain.

_____

_____

_____

Read the problem below. Then explore how to describe the center of a data set using mean, or average.

Anna looked at the survey results for band: {10, 10, 10, 10, 10, 10, 20, 20, 40, 60}

Based on this data, she thinks the average money raised by a band student is $10. What is the mean, or average, of the band data? Is Anna correct? Explain.

You can apply the idea of fair sharing to understand the concept of *mean*.

You can draw a graph to represent the amount of money each student raised.

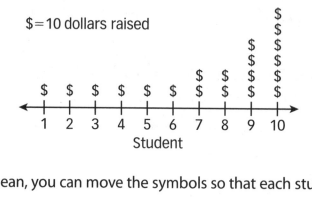

Then, to show the mean, you can move the symbols so that each student raised an equal amount.

You can add the data values and divide by the total number of values to find the mean.

First, add the data points. 10 + 10 + 10 + 10 + 10 + 10 + 20 + 20 + 40 + 60 = 200

Then, divide the sum by the number of values.

Mean = $\frac{200}{10}$

Connect It

Now you will solve the problem and explain how the mean describes the center of a data set.

2 Explain how to find the mean using the first model.

_____

_____

_____

3 Look at the second Model It. What does the 200 represent? The 10? Why do you divide 200 by 10?

_____

_____

4 Are there any outliers in the data? What are they? How do you know?

_____

_____

5 Calculate the mean without outliers.

_____

6 How do outliers affect the mean? Explain.

_____

_____

Try It

Use what you just learned about mean to solve these problems. Show your work on a separate sheet of paper.

7 Here are the chorus data: {0, 10, 10, 20, 20, 20, 20, 30, 30, 40} What is the mean?

_____

8 Here are the strings data: {0, 10, 40, 40, 40, 50, 50, 50, 60, 60} What is the mean?

_____

Read the problem below. Then explore how to describe the center of data sets using median and mode.

You found that the band and chorus data both have a mean of $20. Find the **median,** the middle number, and the **mode,** the most common number, to compare the center of each data set in a different way.

Model It

You can use the median to describe the center of a data set.

To find the **median,** or middle number, you can list and order the data points from least to greatest. Then, you can circle the middle number. Half of the values in a data set are above the median and half below.

?

Band   10, 10, 10, 10, (10, 10,) 20, 20, 40, 60

Chorus   0, 10, 10, 20, (20, 20,) 20, 30, 30, 40

?

When there are two middle numbers, the median is the mean, or average, of the two numbers.

Model It

You can use the mode to describe the center of a data set.

To find the **mode,** or most common number, you can look at the line plots to see which number in each data set appears the most often.

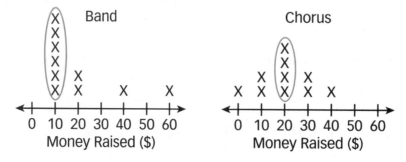

There can be more than one value that appears the most often.

Connect It

Now you will solve the problem using the models and explain how median and mode describe the center of a data set.

9 Look at the first Model It. What is the median for the band data? the chorus data? Explain how you know.

_____

_____

_____

10 Why does it make sense that the mean for the band data is greater than the median?

_____

11 Why do you put the numbers in order from least to greatest to find the median?

_____

_____

12 Look at the second Model It. What is the mode for the band data? the chorus data?

_____

13 Explain the meaning of both the median and the mode within this problem situation.

_____

_____

Try It

Use what you just learned about the median and mode as a measure of center to solve this problem. Show your work on a separate sheet of paper.

14 Look at the strings data. {0, 10, 40, 40, 40, 50, 50, 50, 60, 60} Find the median and mode. Is the mean greater than or less than the median? Explain.

_____

_____

Read the problem below. Then explore how to describe the spread of data sets.

Jess knows the range of any data set is the difference between the highest and lowest values. The range of a data set is a measure of the data set's variability, also called its spread. Is there another way to measure the spread of a data set? If so, how is it done?

Model It

You can find the mean absolute deviation (MAD) to describe the spread of data points from the mean.

Range and MAD describe the variability of a data set in different ways.

- **Range** is the variation of data points between the least and greatest values.

- **MAD** is the average distance of each data point from the mean.

To find the MAD:

1. Find the deviation, or distance, of each data value from the mean.

2. Find the absolute value of the deviation of each data value from the mean.

3. Find the average of these absolute deviations.

Band		
Data Value	Deviation (distance) from Mean	Absolute Deviation
10	−10	10
10	−10	10
10	−10	10
10	−10	10
10	−10	10
10	−10	10
20	0	0
20	0	0
40	20	20
60	40	40
	MAD: $\frac{120}{10} = 12$	

Strings		
Data Value	Deviation (distance) from Mean	Absolute Deviation
0	−40	40
10	−30	30
40	0	0
40	0	0
40	0	0
50	10	10
50	10	10
50	10	10
60	20	20
60	20	20
	MAD: $\frac{140}{10} = 14$	

The MAD of 12 means that, on average, every data point is $12 from the mean.

On average, every data point is $14 from the mean.

Connect It

Now you will solve the problem using the model and describe the spread of data sets.

15 Look at the tables in Model It.

What does a negative deviation mean? _____

What does a positive deviation mean? _____

What does 0 deviation mean? _____

16 Why do you take the absolute value of the deviation?

_____

_____

17 Compare the band and strings MAD values. Which had slightly less variability in data points from the mean? Explain why that might be.

_____

_____

18 Which indicates the greater degree of variability in a data set: A high MAD value or a low MAD value? Explain your answer.

_____

_____

Try It

Use what you just learned about describing the spread of data to solve this problem. Show your work on a separate sheet of paper.

19 Look at the chorus data: {0, 10, 10, 20, 20, 20, 20, 30, 30, 40}

A. Find the range. What does the range mean?

_____

B. The mean is $20. Find the MAD. What does the MAD value mean?

_____

_____

Study the student model below. Then solve problems 20–22.

Student Model

To find the mean, this student added the data values and divided by the total number of data values.

The table below shows the 5 lowest temperatures recorded in the U.S. What is the mean of these data points?

Fort Yukon, Alaska	−80 °F
Medicine Lake, Montana	−70 °F
Saint George, Utah	−69 °F
Basin, Wyoming	−63 °F
Bennett, Colorado	−61 °F

Look at how you can show your work using a model.

Add the data points.

$-80 + (-70) + (-69) + (-63) + (-61) = -343$

Divide by the total number of data values.

$-343 \div 5 = -68.6$

Solution: ___The mean is −68.6 °F_____

💬**Pair/Share**

How is this problem different from the others you've seen in this lesson?

20 15 sixth graders and 15 seventh graders were asked: How many extracurricular activities do you participate in? Here are the survey results:

6th grade {0, 0, 1, 1, 1, 2, 2, 2, 2, 2, 3, 3, 3, 4, 4}
7th grade {1, 1, 1, 1, 1, 3, 3, 3, 3, 3, 4, 4, 4, 4, 4}

Find the mean for each data set. Based on these survey results, in which grade do students participate in more activities?

Show your work.

Look at the numbers in each data set. Can you predict which grade will have a higher mean?

💬**Pair/Share**

What is the median for each grade? How does it compare to the mean?

Solution: _____

_____

_____

21 The line plot below shows how long it took students in a P.E. class to run 1 mile.

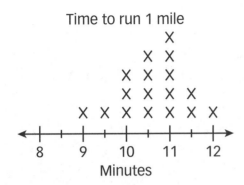

Time to run 1 mile

Describe the shape of the graph.

Solution: _____

_____

_____

What is the difference between a symmetric and a skewed graph?

Pair/Share
Are there any outliers? How do outliers change the center and spread of a graph?

22 Look at the data in the line plot in problem 21. Which of the statements below is FALSE? Circle the letter of the correct answer.

A The median is 10.5

B The mean is 10.5.

C The mode is 11.

D The range is 3.

Lisa chose **A** as the correct answer. Why might Lisa have chosen A?

_____

_____

_____

_____

How can you look at the line plots to find the median, mode, and range?

Pair/Share
How are peak and mode often related when looking at a line plot?

Solve the problems.

1   This data set represents the number of children in 8 families.

4, 2, 1, 2, 4, 2, 6, 3

The mean of this data set is 3. What is the mean absolute deviation (MAD)?

A   1.25   **C**   3.3

B   8   **D**   3

2   Five students scored 80 on a test, five students scored 85, and five students scored 90. Complete each statement below by inserting the correct number.

A   The mean is equal to ☐.

B   The median is equal to ☐.

C   The range is equal to ☐.

D   The mean absolute deviation is equal to ☐.

3   In a statistical study, sixth and seventh graders were asked how many hours of television they watch over the course of a school week. The results are shown below.

	Mean (hr)	Median (hr)	Mean Absolute Deviation (hr)
6th Grade	16.5	18	10
7th Grade	15.75	15	6

Choose True or False for each statement.

A   The mean absolute deviation tells how many students participated from each grade.   ☐ True   ☐ False

B   The data for the 7th graders is likely more concentrated around its mean than the data for the 6th graders.   ☐ True   ☐ False

C   Fifty percent of the 6th graders report that they watch more than 18 hours of television per week.   ☐ True   ☐ False

D   You can determine the range of each set of data just from the information given.   ☐ True   ☐ False

4   In a marketing study, two different groups of 12 people previewed a new movie. They rated the movie from 10, the best, to 1, the worst. The data for each group is shown below.

Group A: 8, 7, 1, 6, 8, 5, 5, 8, 8, 1, 7, 8

Group B: 8, 7, 1, 6, 5, 5, 7, 2, 8, 1, 7, 6

Which statement **must** be true? Circle all that apply.

A   The mode of Group A exceeds the mode of Group B by 1.

B   The mean of Group A exceeds the mean of Group B by 1.

C   The median of Group A is equal to the median of Group B.

D   The range of Group A is equal to the range of Group B.

5   Ten sixth graders were asked two questions. Below are the questions and survey results.

Question 1: How many hours per day do you spend playing outside?

{0, 0, 0, 0, 1, 1, 1, 1, 2, 3}

Question 2: How many hours per day do you spend using an electronic device?

{0, 2, 4, 4, 5, 6, 6, 7, 8, 8}

A   Draw two line plots, one for each set of data. Then describe the shape of each line plot.

_____

_____

_____

B   Find the mean of the data sets.

_____

C   On average, how much more time do sixth graders spend playing with electronic devices than they do playing outside?

_____

_____

 **Self Check**   *Go back and see what you can check off on the Self Check on page 265.*

You've learned how to display data on a line plot. Take a look at this problem.

A random sample of teenagers ages 13 and 14 were asked: On average, how many text messages do you send per day? Here are the results:

0, 10, 10, 10, 10, 20, 20, 20, 30, 50, 50, 50, 90, 100, 100

Display the data in a dot plot. What can you say about the results?

🔍 Explore It

Use the math you already know to solve this problem.

▪ Draw a dot plot to represent the data. Instead of an "x," draw a dot to represent each person's response.

Text Messages Sent per Day

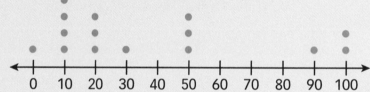
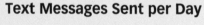

▪ How many teenagers were surveyed? How do you know?

_____

▪ Describe the shape of the graph.

_____

_____

▪ Count the number of dots at 0 and at 10. What do these numbers mean?

_____

▪ What is one conclusion you can draw from this dot plot?

_____

_____

_____

Find Out More

On the previous page, you displayed the data in a dot plot and analyzed the data. Dot plots are best for small data sets. Each dot represents one piece of data in the data set.

Dot plots are one way to display and analyze data. Another way is to put data points into groups. Let's say you were interested in finding out how many teenagers send 50 or more text messages per day and how many send fewer than 50 text messages per day. You can count the number of dots in those categories and make a table.

Text Messages Sent per Day	Number of Responses
0–49	9
50–100	6

Then, you can display the data in a histogram.

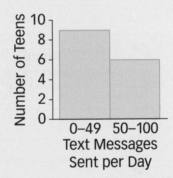

A **histogram** groups the data using intervals, or bins, on a number line. The height of each bar represents the number of data points in that group.

Reflect

1 Explain the difference between a dot plot and a histogram.

_____

_____

_____

_____

Read the problem below. Then explore how to display data in a histogram.

Caroline looked at the text messaging data and drew the histogram to the right. She noticed that this histogram does not show how most of the data points are clustered around 10 and 20 text messages per day.

Draw a histogram to show the data grouped in a different way.

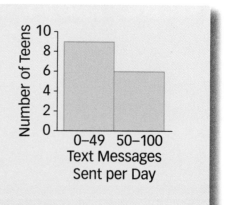

🔍 Model It

You can use more intervals and display the data in a table to help understand this problem.

Text Messages Sent per Day	Number of Teens
0–20	8
21–40	1
41–60	3
61–80	0
81–100	3

🔍 Model It

You can display the data in a histogram to look at the data in another way.

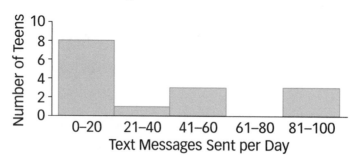

Connect It

Now you will use the models to explain how histograms display data.

2 Look at the histogram in the second Model It. What do the numbers on the vertical axis mean?

_____

What do the numbers on the horizontal axis mean?

_____

3 What does the height of each bar represent?

_____

4 What does it mean that there is no bar at the interval 61–80?

_____

5 Compare the histogram at the top of the previous page with the histogram at the bottom of that page. Which histogram better represents the spread of the data?

Explain. _____

_____

_____

_____

6 How does changing the interval, or bin, size change the way a histogram looks?

_____

_____

Try It

Use what you just learned about histograms to solve this problem.

7 20 sixth graders were asked:
How many potted plants are in your home?

Draw a histogram to represent the data,
which are shown below.

0, 1, 2, 2, 3, 4, 4, 5, 5, 6, 6, 6, 6, 7, 7, 8, 8, 9, 11, 12

Read the problem below. Then explore how to display data in a box plot.

Michelle looks at the text messaging data and wants to describe the spread of numbers above and below the median.

$$0, 10, 10, 10, 10, 20, 20, 20, 30, 50, 50, 50, 90, 100, 100$$

Describe the spread of the data above and below the median.

 **Model It**

You can display the data in a box plot to help you solve this problem.

You can find the median. Then find the upper and lower quartile. The **lower quartile** is the middle number between the minimum and the median. The **upper quartile** is the middle number between the median and maximum.

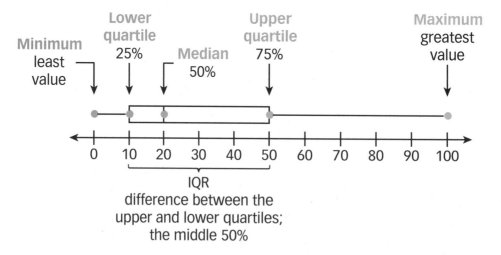

A **box plot** is a 5-number summary.

Another number, the **interquartile range (IQR),** is the difference between the upper quartile and lower quartile. It represents the middle 50% of the data.

Connect It

Now you will solve the problem and explain what the different parts of a box plot mean.

8 What is the median of this data set? What does this number mean?

_____

_____

9 Is there a wider spread above or below the median? Explain.

_____

_____

_____

10 Explain what the length of the rectangular box represents.

_____

11 Explain what the lines extending from the ends of the box represent.

_____

_____

12 What is the IQR of this data set? Does it include outliers?

_____

_____

Try It

Use what you just learned about box plots to solve this problem.

13 Display the data from problem 7 in a box plot. What is the IQR? _____

0, 1, 2, 2, 3, 4, 4, 5, 5, 6, 6, 6, 6, 7, 7, 8, 8, 9, 11, 12

Read the problem below. Then explore how to analyze the data.

The test scores of students in a math class are listed below.

80, 72, 82, 80, 80, 80, 88, 88, 84, 92, 92, 92, 96, 70, 90, 98, 92, 88, 92, 90, 80, 84

Construct a dot plot, histogram, and box plot to display and analyze the data.

Model It

You can display the data in a dot plot.

Test Scores

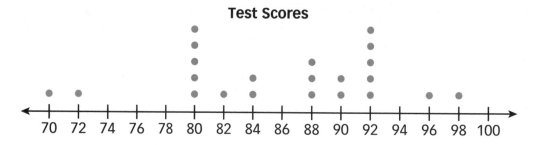

Model It

You can display the data in a histogram.

Test Scores

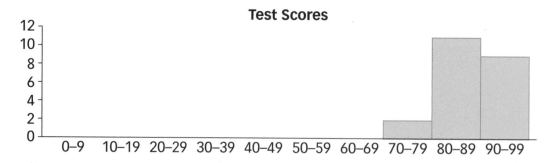

Model It

You can display the data in a box plot.

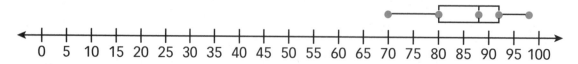

Connect It

Now you will compare the three data displays on the previous page.

14 Which graph is best for finding out the most common test score? Explain.

_____

_____

15 How does drawing a dot plot help order the data values from least to greatest?

_____

_____

16 Explain which graph is best if you want to know how many people scored a B on the test. (In the students' math class, a B is a score from 80 to 89.)

_____

_____

17 Explain which graph is best for a teacher who wants to know the range of scores for the bottom 25%, the middle 50%, and the top 25%.

_____

_____

18 Why is it important to display data in different ways?

_____

_____

Try It

Use what you just learned about analyzing data to solve this problem. Show your work on a separate sheet of paper.

19 Brittany asked her classmates: How much time, in minutes, do you spend reading each day? Here are the results: 10, 20, 20, 20, 30, 30, 30, 30, 30, 40, 40, 40, 60, 60, 60.

Display the data in a dot plot, a histogram, and a box plot. Next to each graph, write down something you notice about the data.

The student ordered the temperatures from least to greatest and found the minimum, lower quartile, median, upper quarter, and maximum.

Study the student model below. Then solve problems 20–22.

Jenny recorded the temperature (°F) for 20 days this winter.

58	58	52	50	50	48	52	40	35	40
35	32	40	32	30	28	20	24	18	18

Draw a box plot to represent the data.

Look at how you can show your work.

           29   37.5   50
18, 18, 20, 24, 28, 30, 32, 32, 35, 35, 40, 40, 40, 48, 50, 50, 52, 52, 58, 58

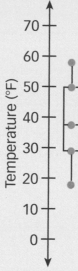

Pair/Share

How is this box plot different from the others in this lesson?

How many dots will be on this dot plot?

20 Display the temperatures from the student model in a dot plot.

Pair/Share

Is the dot plot skewed or symmetrical? Are there any outliers?

21 Look at the temperatures from the student model problem.

First, complete the table below.

Temperatures (°F)	Number of Days
0–9	
10–19	
20–29	
30–39	
40–49	
50–59	

Now, use the table to draw a histogram that represents the data. Remember to label your axes.

How many temperatures are in each interval?

Pair/Share

Why might you notice a skew in the histogram more than in the dot plot?

22 Which of the following questions can be answered using the histogram you drew in problem 21?

A How many days was the temperature below freezing (32°F)?

B How many days was the temperature above 50°F?

C What is the median temperature?

D What were the highest and lowest temperatures recorded?

Felix chose **A** as the correct answer. Explain why the histogram cannot answer that question.

_____

_____

_____

Which question asks about the number of days for a certain group of temperatures?

Pair/Share

Choose the question that can be answered and explain why.

Solve the problems.

1 The box plot below represents the heights of the basketball players on a college team.

Basketball Players' Heights

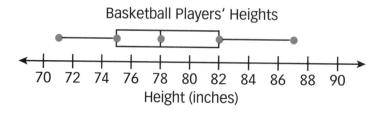

Height (inches)

What percent of basketball players are taller than 82 inches?

A   25%

B   50%

C   75%

D   100%

2 The list of numbers represents the weight, in pounds, of players on a college football team.

170, 175, 188, 188, 190, 192, 193, 193, 193, 197, 230

Write the appropriate value in each box below the box plot.

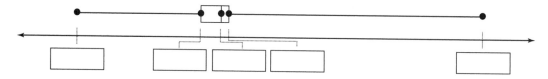

3 The following are the approximate weights, in grams, of 14 bullfrogs caught one afternoon.

460, 470, 480, 480, 480, 490, 490, 490, 490, 490, 490, 500, 500, 510

Create a dot plot to display the data.

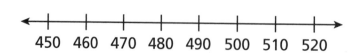

450   460   470   480   490   500   510   520

4   A crayon factory recorded the number of broken crayons per box in a dot plot.

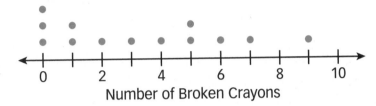

Number of Broken Crayons

Part A

Construct a histogram that shows both the number of boxes and the number of broken crayons.

Part B

Look at the histogram you made in Part A. Describe at least one advantage a histogram has over a dot plot when it comes to displaying the crayon factory's data.

_____

_____

_____

_____

✓ **Self Check**   *Go back and see what you can check off on the Self Check on page 265.*

Lesson 29   Part 1: Introduction 👥

Analyze Numerical Data

You've learned how to measure the center of data values with median and mean. Take a look at this problem.

Death Valley National Park in the western United States is known for its extreme temperatures. This table shows high temperatures for the first 15 days of October.

99°F	113°F	99°F	97°F	91°F
88°F	88°F	90°F	84°F	81°F
71°F	80°F	79°F	84°F	96°F

Use median and mean to describe the data.

🔍 Explore It

Use the math you already know to solve this problem.

◼ Construct a dot plot.

Death Valley National Park High Temperatures

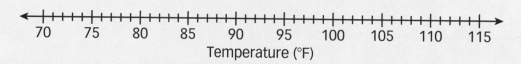

Temperature (°F)

◼ Describe the shape of the data. What does the shape tell you about the temperatures?

_____

_____

◼ Do you notice any outliers? Explain. _____

_____

◼ What is the median temperature? _____ mean? _____

◼ What's similar about the mean and median? What's different? Explain. _____

_____

_____

Find Out More

What would happen to the median and mean if you eliminate the outlier and replace it with a less extreme temperature, like 100°F?

The data set and dot plot would look like this:

99°F	100°F	99°F	97°F	91°F
88°F	88°F	90°F	84°F	81°F
71°F	80°F	79°F	84°F	96°F

Death Valley National Park High Temperatures

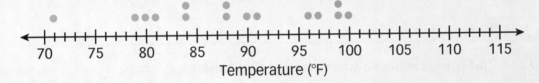

Temperature (°F)

The median does not change; it is still 88°F. The mean changes from about 89.3°F to about 88.5°F. In this context, the outlier influences the mean but not the median.

Reflect

1 Explain why outliers affect the mean.

_____

_____

_____

_____

Read the problem below. Then explore how the interquartile range (IQR) measures variability.

Consider the first set of Death Valley National Park temperatures that you saw. What does the interquartile range (IQR) tell you about the variability of the temperatures?

99°F	113°F	99°F	97°F	91°F
88°F	88°F	90°F	84°F	81°F
71°F	80°F	79°F	84°F	96°F

🔍 Model It

You can find the quartile values to understand the problem.

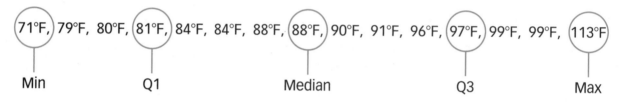

71°F, 79°F, 80°F, 81°F, 84°F, 84°F, 88°F, 88°F, 90°F, 91°F, 96°F, 97°F, 99°F, 99°F, 113°F

Min   Q1   Median   Q3   Max

🔍 Model It

You can draw a box plot to understand the problem.

Death Valley National Park High Temperatures

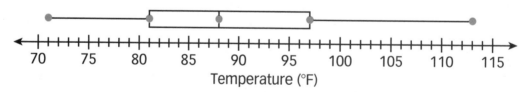

Temperature (°F)

Connect It

Now you will solve the problem using the models.

2 Calculate the IQR. What does it mean within this context?

_____

_____

3 Look at the box plot. How many data points are represented by the box? What does this box mean?

_____

_____

4 If you replace the outlier (113°F) with 100°F, what happens to the IQR? What happens to the range? Explain.

_____

_____

_____

5 Within this context, explain what the median and the IQR tell you about the data.

_____

_____

Try It

Use what you just learned about median and IQR to solve this problem. Show your work on a separate sheet of paper.

6 Are the median and IQR typically affected by outliers? Explain.

_____

_____

_____

_____

Read the problem below. Then explore how the Mean Absolute Deviation (MAD) measures variability.

Consider another way to describe the Death Valley National Park temperature data. Calculate the mean absolute deviation (MAD). What does the MAD tell you about the variability of the temperatures?

99°F	113°F	99°F	97°F	91°F
88°F	88°F	90°F	84°F	81°F
71°F	80°F	79°F	84°F	96°F

 **Model It**

You can make a table to understand the problem.

Data Value	Deviation from Mean Mean = 89.3°F	Absolute Deviation
99°F	9.7	9.7
88°F	−1.3	1.3
71°F	−18.3	18.3
113°F	23.7	23.7
88°F	−1.3	1.3
80°F	−9.3	9.3
99°F	9.7	9.7
90°F	0.7	0.7
79°F	−10.3	10.3
97°F	7.7	7.7
84°F	−5.3	5.3
84°F	−5.3	5.3
91°F	1.7	1.7
81°F	−8.3	8.3
96°F	6.7	6.7
		MAD: $\frac{119.3}{15} = 7.95$

Connect It

Now you will solve the problem using the model.

7 What does the MAD mean within this context?

_____

8 Given this context, does the MAD value indicate a high or low variability?

_____

_____

_____

9 If you replace the outlier (113°F) with 100°F, what happens to the MAD? Explain.

_____

_____

10 Within this context, how are the mean and the MAD different? How are they related?

_____

_____

_____

_____

Try It

Use what you just learned about mean and MAD to answer this question.

11 Are the mean and MAD typically affected by outliers? Explain.

_____

_____

_____

_____

Study the student model below. Then solve problems 12–14.

The student recognized how an outlier can affect a measure of center.

Student Model

Zoe and her lab partners have a mystery mineral that they are trying to identify. They take turns finding the mass of the same mineral before finding its density. Here are their measurements:

50.1 g, 50.4 g, 20.5 g, 50.2 g, 50.2 g

Given this context and these data points, is the median or the mean a better measure of center?

Look at how you could show your work.

20.5   50.1   (50.2)   50.2   50.4

The median, 50.2, is a better measure of data because all of the masses except one are around 50 g. Finding the mean with an outlier such as 20.5 would produce a number much lower than the mineral's actual mass.

◻ Pair/Share

How could you justify your answer with a graph of the data?

Does the outlier affect the mean or the median?

12 Use the data set in the student model above to calculate the mean and the median without the outlier. Now which is a better measure of center? Explain.

Show your work.

◻ Pair/Share

Given this context, why does it make sense to measure the center without the outlier?

Solution: _____

_____

13 Complete the table below. How many data points are represented in this histogram?

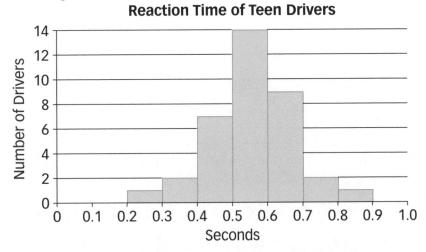

Reaction Time of Teen Drivers

How many data points are in each interval?

Intervals (seconds)	Number of Drivers
	TOTAL =

Pair/Share

In what interval are most of the data values clustered? Does this make sense given the context?

14 Look at the histogram in problem 13. Which of the following statements do you know to be TRUE?

A The data are skewed.

B The median is 0.55 seconds.

C The range is 0.7 seconds.

D The center of the data is between 0.5 to 0.6 seconds.

Jo chose **B** as the correct answer. How did she get that answer?

_____

_____

How do histograms show center and variability?

Pair/Share

How can you help Jo understand her error?

Solve the problems.

1   Look at the box plots. Which is a TRUE statement?

Average Time Spent on Homework

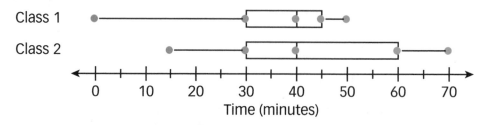

A   If you moved the students from the top 25% in Class 1 into Class 2, the Class 2 median would increase.

B   If you omitted the student(s) who did no homework in Class 1, the IQR for Class 1 would increase.

C   If you combined the data from both classes onto one box plot, the range would be 105.

D   If you combined the data from both classes onto one box plot, the median would be double the current median for Class 1.

2   The cumulative frequency histogram represents the number of minutes per school week that 320 students watch television.

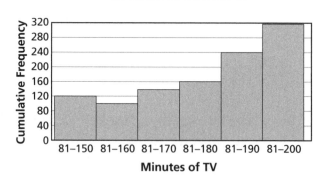

What fraction of the population watches 150 minutes or less of television? ☐

What fraction of the population watches 180 minutes or less of television? ☐

What fraction of the population watches 190 minutes or less of television? ☐

3   This table represents daily attendance at 2 movie theaters for one week.

	Theater 1	Theater 2
Monday	42	24
Tuesday	50	28
Wednesday	48	20
Thursday	60	92
Friday	80	88
Saturday	212	95
Sunday	65	90

Part A

Calculate the mean and median for each theater's attendance. Round your answers to the nearest whole number.

Theater 1:   Mean _____   Median _____

Theater 2:   Mean _____   Median _____

Part B

Which is a better measure of center for Theater 1, mean or median? Explain.

_____

_____

_____

Part C

Which is a better measure of center for Theater 2, mean or median? Explain.

_____

_____

 ✓ **Self Check**   *Go back and see what you can check off on the Self Check on page 265.*

Solve the problems.

1 A park ranger measures the heights of 7 trees. She represents their heights in the box plot.

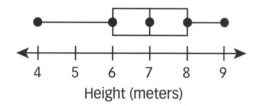

Height (meters)

Which list shows the possible tree heights, in meters, of all 7 trees?

A 4, 5, 7, 7, 8, 8, 9

B 4, 5, 7, 7, 7, 8, 9

C 4, 6, 6, 7, 7, 8, 9

D 4, 6, 7, 7, 8, 8, 9

2 The line plot shows the high temperatures near a school over 8 days.

High Temperature over 8 Days

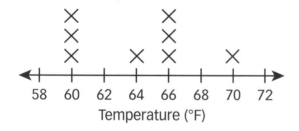

Temperature (°F)

What is the median high temperature?

A 60°F   **C** 65°F

B 64°F   **D** 66°F

3 From the list of numbers below, write one number in each box. You may use each number exactly once.

| 3 |
| 4 |
| 7 |
| 8 |
| 9 |
| 14 |

Three unique numbers with mean = 8 and MAD = 4

☐ ☐ ☐

Three unique numbers with mean = 7 and MAD = 2

☐ ☐ ☐

4 Which question could have variability in the data related to it? Circle all that apply.

A How many board games does Michelle own?

B When does Melissa's lunch hour begin?

C How many books has each student read this year?

D How tall is Blake?

E What are the favorite colors among the 6th-grade students?

5 Callie kept track of the times for her classmates in a 600-meter run. Four of her classmates finished in less than 2 minutes, 9 finished with times between 2 minutes and 3 minutes, 6 finished with times between 3 minutes and 4 minutes, and 3 finished with times greater than 4 minutes.

In the space below, draw a histogram to display Callie's data. Be sure to label your histogram and give it a title.

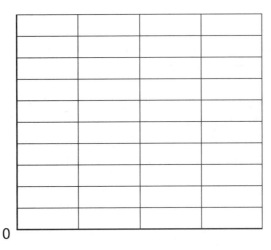

6 Rosa's dog had three puppies. After a few months, she measured the weight of the four dogs. The weights were 16 pounds, 18.5 pounds, 60 pounds, and 19.5 pounds.

Part A

Which of the four weights is an outlier? What is the *most likely* explanation for the outlier?

_____

_____

Part B

How much greater is the mean weight of the four dogs than the mean weight of three dogs without the outlier?

Show your work.

Answer _____ pounds

Performance Task

Answer the questions and show all your work on separate paper.

Andrea gathered the following data from students in her class:

Name	Jack	Roy	Lee	Jasmine	Pablo	Bob	Yvonne	Tia
Amount	5	7	4	8	5	19	6	6

A. Examine the numbers she recorded. Then write a statistical question that Andrea may have been trying to answer.

B. Construct a dot plot of Andrea's data. Use the dot plot to describe the shape, center, and spread of the data.

C. Andrea used software to make a box plot and histogram for her data:

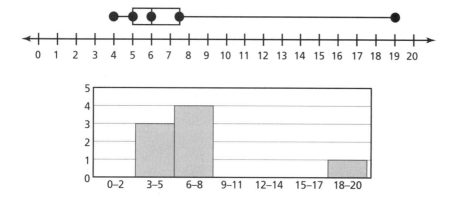

Which graph is the best visual model for measures of center? Which graph is the best visual model for the measure of variability? Explain your choices.

Reflect on Mathematical Practices

After you complete the task, choose one of the following questions to answer.

1. **Reason Mathematically** How did you justify your choices of data displays?

2. **Model** Which of the three graphs was the least useful for analyzing this set of data?

Common Core State Standards for Mathematics, Grade 6

The chart below correlates each Common Core State Standard to the *Ready® Common Core Instruction* lesson(s) that offer(s) comprehensive instruction on that standard. Use this chart to determine which lessons your students should complete based on their mastery of each standard.

Common Core State Standards for Grade 6 — Mathematics Standards	Content Emphasis	Ready® Common Core Instruction Lesson(s)
Ratios and Proportional Relationships		
Understand ratio concepts and use ratio reasoning to solve problems.		
6.RP.A.1 Understand the concept of a ratio and use ratio language to describe a ratio relationship between two quantities. *For example, "The ratio of wings to beaks in the bird house at the zoo was 2:1, because for every 2 wings there was 1 beak." "For every vote candidate A received, candidate C received nearly three votes."*	Major	1
6.RP.A.2 Understand the concept of a unit rate $\frac{a}{b}$ associated with a ratio $a{:}b$ with $b \neq 0$, and use rate language in the context of a ratio relationship. *For example, "This recipe has a ratio of 3 cups of flour to 4 cups of sugar, so there is $\frac{3}{4}$ cup of flour for each cup of sugar." "We paid $75 for 15 hamburgers, which is a rate of $5 per hamburger.*	Major	2
6.RP.A.3 Use ratio and rate reasoning to solve real-world and mathematical problems, e.g., by reasoning about tables of equivalent ratios, tape diagrams, double number line diagrams, or equations.	Major	3, 4, 5
6.RP.A.3a Make tables of equivalent ratios relating quantities with whole-number measurements, find missing values in the tables, and plot the pairs of values on the coordinate plane. Use tables to compare ratios.	Major	3
6.RP.A.3b Solve unit rate problems including those involving unit pricing and constant speed. *For example, if it took 7 hours to mow 4 lawns, then at that rate, how many lawns could be mowed in 35 hours? At what rate were lawns being mowed?*	Major	4
6.RP.A.3c Find a percent of a quantity as a rate per 100 (e.g., 30% of a quantity means $\frac{30}{100}$ times the quantity); solve problems involving finding the whole, given a part and the percent.	Major	5
6.RP.A.3d Use ratio reasoning to convert measurement units; manipulate and transform units appropriately when multiplying or dividing quantities.	Major	4
The Number System		
Apply and extend previous understandings of multiplication and division to divide fractions by fractions.		
6.NS.A.1 Interpret and compute quotients of fractions, and solve word problems involving division of fractions by fractions, e.g., by using visual fraction models and equations to represent the problem. *For example, create a story context for $\left(\frac{2}{3}\right) \div \left(\frac{3}{4}\right)$ and use a visual fraction model to show the quotient; use the relationship between multiplication and division to explain that $\left(\frac{2}{3}\right) \div \left(\frac{3}{4}\right) = \frac{8}{9}$ because $\frac{3}{4}$ of $\frac{8}{9}$ is $\frac{2}{3}$. (In general, $\left(\frac{a}{b}\right) \div \left(\frac{c}{d}\right) = \frac{ad}{bc}$.) How much chocolate will each person get if 3 people share $\frac{1}{2}$ lb of chocolate equally? How many $\frac{3}{4}$-cup servings are in $\frac{2}{3}$ of a cup of yogurt? How wide is a rectangular strip of land with length $\frac{3}{4}$ mi and area $\frac{1}{2}$ square mi?*	Major	6, 7
Compute fluently with multi-digit numbers and find common factors and multiples.		
6.NS.B.2 Fluently divide multi-digit numbers using the standard algorithm.	Supporting/ Additional	8

The Standards for Mathematical Practice are integrated throughout the instructional lessons.

Common Core State Standards for Grade 6 — Mathematics Standards	Content Emphasis	Ready® Common Core Instruction Lesson(s)
The Number System (*continued*)		
Compute fluently with multi-digit numbers and find common factors and multiples. (*continued*)		
6.NS.B.3 Fluently add, subtract, multiply, and divide multi-digit decimals using the standard algorithm for each operation.	Supporting/ Additional	9, 10
6.NS.B.4 Find the greatest common factor of two whole numbers less than or equal to 100 and the least common multiple of two whole numbers less than or equal to 12. Use the distributive property to express a sum of two whole numbers 1–100 with a common factor as a multiple of a sum of two whole numbers with no common factor. *For example, express 36 + 8 as 4(9 + 2).*	Supporting/ Additional	11
Apply and extend previous understandings of numbers to the system of rational numbers.		
6.NS.C.5 Understand that positive and negative numbers are used together to describe quantities having opposite directions or values (e.g., temperature above/below zero, elevation above/below sea level, credits/debits, positive/negative electric charge); use positive and negative numbers to represent quantities in real-world contexts, explaining the meaning of 0 in each situation.	Major	12, 13
6.NS.C.6 Understand a rational number as a point on the number line. Extend number line diagrams and coordinate axes familiar from previous grades to represent points on the line and in the plane with negative number coordinates.	Major	12, 14
6.NS.C.6a Recognize opposite signs of numbers as indicating locations on opposite sides of 0 on the number line; recognize that the opposite of the opposite of a number is the number itself, e.g., $-(-3) = 3$, and that 0 is its own opposite.	Major	12
6.NS.C.6b Understand signs of numbers in ordered pairs as indicating locations in quadrants of the coordinate plane; recognize that when two ordered pairs differ only by signs, the locations of the points are related by reflections across one or both axes.	Major	14
6.NS.C.6c Find and position integers and other rational numbers on a horizontal or vertical number line diagram; find and position pairs of integers and other rational numbers on a coordinate plane.	Major	12, 14
6.NS.C.7 Understand ordering and absolute value of rational numbers.	Major	13
6.NS.C.7a Interpret statements of inequality as statements about the relative position of two numbers on a number line diagram. *For example, interpret $-3 > -7$ as a statement that -3 is located to the right of -7 on a number line oriented from left to right.*	Major	13
6.NS.C.7b Write, interpret, and explain statements of order for rational numbers in real-world contexts. *For example, write $-3°C > -7°C$ to express the fact that $-3°C$ is warmer than $-7°C$.*	Major	13
6.NS.C.7c Understand the absolute value of a rational number as its distance from 0 on the number line; interpret absolute value as magnitude for a positive or negative quantity in a real-world situation. *For example, for an account balance of -30 dollars, write $|-30| = 30$ to describe the size of the debt in dollars.*	Major	13
6.NS.C.7d Distinguish comparisons of absolute value from statements about order. *For example, recognize that an account balance less than -30 dollars represents a debt greater than 30 dollars.*	Major	13
6.NS.C.8 Solve real-world and mathematical problems by graphing points in all four quadrants of the coordinate plane. Include use of coordinates and absolute value to find distances between points with the same first coordinate or the same second coordinate.	Major	14
Expressions and Equations		
Apply and extend previous understandings of arithmetic to algebraic expressions.		
6.EE.A.1 Write and evaluate numerical expressions involving whole-number exponents.	Major	15
6.EE.A.2 Write, read, and evaluate expressions in which letters stand for numbers.	Major	16
6.EE.A.2a Write expressions that record operations with numbers and with letters standing for numbers. *For example, express the calculation "Subtract y from 5" as $5 - y$.*	Major	16

The Standards for Mathematical Practice are integrated throughout the instructional lessons.

Common Core State Standards for Grade 6 — Mathematics Standards	Content Emphasis	Ready® Common Core Instruction Lesson(s)
Expressions and Equations *(continued)*		
Apply and extend previous understandings of arithmetic to algebraic expressions. *(continued)*		
6.EE.A.2b Identify parts of an expression using mathematical terms (sum, term, product, factor, quotient, coefficient); view one or more parts of an expression as a single entity. *For example, describe the expression 2(8 + 7) as a product of two factors; view (8 + 7) as both a single entity and a sum of two terms.*	Major	16
6.EE.A.2c Evaluate expressions at specific values of their variables. Include expressions that arise from formulas used in real-world problems. Perform arithmetic operations, including those involving whole-number exponents, in the conventional order when there are no parentheses to specify a particular order (Order of Operations). *For example, use the formulas $V = s^3$ and $A = 6s^2$ to find the volume and surface area of a cube with sides of length $s = \frac{1}{2}$.*	Major	16
6.EE.A.3 Apply the properties of operations to generate equivalent expressions. *For example, apply the distributive property to the expression $3(2 + x)$ to produce the equivalent expression $6 + 3x$; apply the distributive property to the expression $24x + 18y$ to produce the equivalent expression $6(4x + 3y)$; apply properties of operations to $y + y + y$ to produce the equivalent expression $3y$.*	Major	17
6.EE.A.4 Identify when two expressions are equivalent (ie., when the two expressions name the same number regardless of which value is substituted into them). *For example, the expressions $y + y + y$ and $3y$ are equivalent because they name the same number regardless of which number y stands for.*	Major	17
Reason about and solve one-variable equations and inequalities.		
6.EE.B.5 Understand solving an equation or inequality as a process of answering a question: which values from a specified set, if any, make the equation or inequality true? Use substitution to determine whether a given number in a specified set makes an equation or inequality true.	Major	18, 20
6.EE.B.6 Use variables to represent numbers and write expressions when solving a real-world or mathematical problem; understand that a variable can represent an unknown number, or, depending on the purpose at hand, any number in a specified set.	Major	19
6.EE.B.7 Solve real-world and mathematical problems by writing and solving equations of the form $x + p = q$ and $px = q$ for cases in which p, q and x are all nonnegative rational numbers.	Major	19
6.EE.B.8 Write an inequality of the form $x > c$ or $x < c$ to represent a constraint or condition in a real-world or mathematical problem. Recognize that inequalities of the form $x > c$ or $x < c$ have infinitely many solutions; represent solutions of such inequalities on number line diagrams.	Major	20
Represent and analyze quantitative relationships between dependent and independent variables.		
6.EE.C.9 Use variables to represent two quantities in a real-world problem that change in relationship to one another; write an equation to express one quantity, thought of as the dependent variable, in terms of the other quantity, thought of as the independent variable. Analyze the relationship between the dependent and independent variables using graphs and tables, and relate these to the equation. *For example, in a problem involving motion at constant speed, list and graph ordered pairs of distances and times, and write the equation $d = 65t$ to represent the relationship between distance and time.*	Major	21

The Standards for Mathematical Practice are integrated throughout the instructional lessons.

Common Core State Standards for Grade 6 — Mathematics Standards	Content Emphasis	Ready® Common Core Instruction Lesson(s)
Geometry		
Solve real-world and mathematical problems involving area, surface area, and volume.		
6.G.A.1 Find the area of right triangles, other triangles, special quadrilaterals, and polygons by composing into rectangles or decomposing into triangles and other shapes; apply these techniques in the context of solving real-world and mathematical problems.	Supporting/ Additional	22
6.G.A.2 Find the volume of a right rectangular prism with fractional edge lengths by packing it with unit cubes of the appropriate unit fraction edge lengths, and show that the volume is the same as would be found by multiplying the edge lengths of the prism. Apply the formulas $V = lwh$ and $V = bh$ to find volumes of right rectangular prisms with fractional edge lengths in the context of solving real-world and mathematical problems.	Supporting/ Additional	25
6.G.A.3 Draw polygons in the coordinate plane given coordinates for the vertices; use coordinates to find the length of a side joining points with the same first coordinate or the same second coordinate. Apply these techniques in the context of solving real-world and mathematical problems.	Supporting/ Additional	23
6.G.A.4 Represent three-dimensional figures using nets made up of rectangles and triangles, and use the nets to find the surface area of these figures. Apply these techniques in the context of solving real-world and mathematical problems.	Supporting/ Additional	24
Statistics and Probability		
Develop understanding of statistical variability.		
6.SP.A.1 Recognize a statistical question as one that anticipates variability in the data related to the question and accounts for it in the answers. *For example, "How old am I?" is not a statistical question, but "How old are the students in my school?" is a statistical question because one anticipates variability in students' ages.*	Supporting/ Additional	26
6.SP.A.2 Understand that a set of data collected to answer a statistical question has a distribution which can be described by its center, spread, and overall shape.	Supporting/ Additional	27
6.SP.A.3 Recognize that a measure of center for a numerical data set summarizes all of its values with a single number, while a measure of variation describes how its values vary with a single number.	Supporting/ Additional	27
Summarize and describe distributions.		
6.SP.B.4 Display numerical data in plots on a number line, including dot plots, histograms, and box plots.	Supporting/ Additional	28
6.SP.B.5 Summarize numerical data sets in relation to their context, such as by:	Supporting/ Additional	29
6.SP.B.5a Reporting the number of observations.	Supporting/ Additional	29
6.SP.B.5b Describing the nature of the attribute under investigation, including how it was measured and its units of measurement.	Supporting/ Additional	29
6.SP.B.5c Giving quantitative measures of center (median and/or mean) and variability (interquartile range and/or mean absolute deviation), as well as describing any overall pattern and any striking deviations from the overall pattern with reference to the context in which the data were gathered.	Supporting/ Additional	29
6.SP.B.5d Relating the choice of measures of center and variability to the shape of the data distribution and the context in which the data were gathered.	Supporting/ Additional	29

The Standards for Mathematical Practice are integrated throughout the instructional lessons.